Handwriting Analysis

The Complete Basic Book

by

KAREN AMEND & MARY S. RUIZ

NEW PAGE BOOKS
A division of The Career Press, Inc.
Franklin Lakes, NJ

HANDWRITING ANALYSIS
ISBN 0-87877-050-X
Printed in the U.S.A. by Book-mart Press

To order this title, please call toll-free 1-800-CAREER-1 (NJ and Canada: 201-848-0310) to order using VISA or MasterCard, or for further information on books from Career Press.

The Career Press, Inc., 3 Tice Road, PO Box 687, Franklin Lakes, NJ 07417

The author of this book does not dispense medical advice nor prescribe the use of any technique as a form of treatment for medical problems without the advice of a physician, either directly or indirectly. The intent of the author is only to offer information of a general nature to help you cooperate with your doctor in your mutual quest for health. In the event you use any of the information in this book for yourself, you are prescribing for yourself, which is your constitutional right, but the author and publisher assume no responsibility for your actions.

Library of Congress Cataloging-in-Publication information available upon request.

To the Reader:
The authors and editors of this manual have taken painstaking efforts to maintain the anonymity and rights of privacy of all persons whose handwriting samples appear herein. With respect to the handwriting samples of any person who is not a public figure, such samples may in fact have been altered, for purposes of concealing their identity, and will not necessarily be actual examples of any person's true penmanship. Notwithstanding this, if it occurs that any person is thought to be identified, on the basis of any handwriting sample contained herein, the reader should bear in mind that the text accompanying each respective sample represents only the authors' analysis of said sample, based on generally accepted graphological principles, and makes no comment on the character of any real person.

Introduction

In this closing quarter of the 20th century, we live in an era emphasizing the achievement of inner peace and harmony. Institutions, groups and individuals have dedicated themselves to helping others attain personal enlightenment and self awareness; synthesizing the mind and body into one smoothly functioning unit is the goal. Physical well-being is an indication of mental well-being, yet when we speak of the healthy individual, we refer to more than the appearance of a trim, active and disease-free body. Some people have the ability to mask their mental and emotional instabilities with an external personality facade designed to give an impression of inner balance. Occasionally the facade is so complete that even the person himself is fooled and the communication with deeper needs and feelings is lost. The outer behavior protects the vulnerable self within; the individual has succeeded in constructing a protective shield against the pain of negative experience.

While we cannot read minds, we can see certain body movements. Tone of voice, gestures, posture, body structure and manner of dress can be interpreted as clues to inner psychological make-up and behavior. Often, the outer style reflects the inner one. It is possible through thoughtful observation to penetrate the disguise and reveal the inner character behind the mask.

Certain facial expressions are associated with certain moods. We can watch a conversation taking place inside a telephone booth and without a sound escaping, still sense the mood of the conversation. The caller tells all with facial expressions and body posture. Thus we demonstrate thoughts and feelings through the silent yet expressive language of our bodies. Handwriting, too, is an expressive and silent gesture.

As you write you are consciously attempting a message. Beyond the conscious information contained in the written words, the handwriting also divulges information about you and how you felt unconsciously as you wrote.

Writing is a physical process. The brain sends an order through the nervous system to the arm, hand and fingers, where together they manipulate the writing tool. In this way, the intent to write forms deep within the creative processes of the mind and makes writing an expressive gesture representative of the mind behind the pen. Despite the teaching of a standard letter model to form the letters and words necessary to express our ideas, no two writings are exactly alike. An American statistician determined that the possibility of two writings being identical is one chance in 68 trillion!

Every written sample displays the same wonderful variety as the faces, finger-prints, voices and bodies of us all. We recognize our friends' voices on the phone, and by the tone alone know their state of happiness or sadness, anger or warmth. Handwriting is a reflection of mood changes, characterizing the writer's state of mind at that moment.

Emotional factors dictate the form of the writing stroke. It is possible to deter-mine personal behavior by studying the mannerisms of formation and spacing within a writing. Handwriting matures, grows or disintegrates along with the per-sonality, or with physical changes due to age, health, or tension. Personality devel-opment can be studied by examining samples penned at various times through the years. These examples provide a visual history of the development of a life emo-tionally, physically and mentally.

The word "graphology" is a combination of the Greek word *graphein*, which means "to write," and the suffix "ology," a branch of scientific study. Graphology, then, is the study of writing based on a growing body of knowledge which is con-stantly being tested in practical use. Since it is a continuing and growing body of knowledge, and not a codified system like basic arithmetic, the student should not be alarmed to find varying, sometimes conflicting interpretations assigned to a stroke or shape. It is possible to understand writing character using different ap-proaches to the specific origins, just as the medical and psychological fields get re-sults even when starting from different positions. And like medicine, graphology is also an art of combining and synthesizing information that requires training and judgment in its application. This book gives the most widely accepted and most practical basic elements of graphology and their meanings. At the end of the book, you will find tips and guidelines for doing your own analyses.

People study handwriting for various reasons. For example, the science of crim-inology offers courses of study which entitle one to be licensed as a handwriting expert. Testimony of the handwriting expert is admissable in a court of law for pur-poses of establishing identification or validity of a particular document. The profes-sional title for one qualified in this field is "examiner of questioned documents." These experts work in cooperation with law enforcement agencies, attorneys or anyone interested in determining officially who wrote what, where and under what conditions. Famous trial cases have involved the services of a handwriting expert to help determine guilt or innocence of the defendant, just as such trials have involved psychologists and psychiatrists.

There is another, larger group of people who study handwriting as a means to discover themselves and others. These people are called graphologists. They know that exaggerations in writing formations suggest similar exaggerations in the per-sonality of the writer. Character traits that deviate from the norm will show up in the handwriting. The graphologist learns to analyze the difference between normal and abnormal traits in the writing. Both fundamental knowledge and interpretive skill have their importance in an accurate analysis of a handwriting sample, and all interpreters unavoidably bring their own personal shadings and colorings to the portrait. The realm of the mind is a subjective area of study. Any kind of psycho-analytic diagnosis or therapy presents the same problem of subjectivity. Handwriting analysis is not infallible.

The systematic and critical study of our bodies and minds teaches us about ourselves. We take blood samples to look for possible negative elements in the body and biopsies to test for possible malignancy. These examples could continue, but the point is that analyzing specific information helps us to understand ourselves.

Writing is initially motivated by the mind. The intricate nerve-muscle interplay necessary to accomplish the writing task originates in the central nervous system. Therefore the study of writing has its analytical importance in dealing with both the mind and the body. Medical science is demonstrating new interest in the clues handwriting provides to physical illness or abnormality. In the past, the medical focus has been to determine what changes emotional and mental disorders cause in handwriting. Now there are handwriting tests that discriminate between certain medical disorders, such as shaking palsy and Parkinson's Disease or between the hardening of the arteries that nourish the brain and those that feed the heart. Handwriting analysis can distinguish between those crippled with arthritis and those suffering from high blood pressure. Other diseases that indicate a loss of nerve control over fine muscular coordination are tuberculosis, cancer, some psychoses, epilepsy, alcoholism and drug addiction. Such factors as the appearance of a tremor in the writing stroke, changes in pressure or inking patterns, and rigidity or loss of free flow within the writing are indicative of such physical illnesses within the writer.

Graphology dynamically enlarges its scope in combination with insights from other projective techniques. It is now widely applied as an additional diagnostic tool by psychologists and psychiatrists who have found it as helpful as the famed Rorschach inkblot test. The structural ambiguity of the Rorschach inkblots allows a wide variety of interpretation for both patient and psychologist. This is also the case with handwriting when writers unconsciously choose the movements and formations characteristic of their state of mind at that time, and the graphologists draw conclusions on the basis of their training.

The academic community resists acceptance of graphology—perhaps because the scientific mind is most comfortable applying sequential thinking to a one-directed end. Students of graphology must by necessity broaden their scope of appraisal from a narrow, linear focus to one of more diversity which provides an understanding of the nature of pattern thinking. Creative minds are more comfortable with the idea that the whole is greater than the sum of its parts and gain advantage through their ability to easily appraise pattern qualities. It is due to a few particularly visionary academicians that graphology has gained its admittedly tenuous footholds in its climb toward deserved respect within the American college and university systems. Interesting to note is the fact that graphology has been part of the accredited curriculum in the psychology departments of universities in France, Germany and Switzerland since the end of the 19th century.

Toward the hope that you the reader will discover an unexplored area within yourself and come to a closer understanding of yourself and others, we inscribe this book.

Karen K Amend   Mary S. Ruiz

Contents

YOUR OWN WRITING: A LAST NAIVE SAMPLE

Write a letter to yourself of at least two paragraphs. The verbal content of your message is unimportant, so just relax and write in your usual style with no pretenses. If you often print or have more than one style of writing, provide a sample of these as well. Sign and date your sample. Remember, the more you write now, the happier you'll be later to have this last unbiased sample.

INTRODUCTION TO HANDWRITING ANALYSIS
GRAPHOLOGY PICTOGRAPHS

THE PAGE REPRESENTS THE AREA OF SPACE SURROUNDING THE WRITER. IT IS HIS ARENA FOR POTENTIAL ACTION.

THE WRITING STROKES SHOW THE TRACK OF THE CONSCIOUS AND UNCONSCIOUS MIND AS EACH ACTS UPON THE AVAILABLE LIFE SPACE.

THE WRITING CHARACTERISTICS WHICH ARE DEFINED BELOW COMBINE WITH ONE ANOTHER IN ANY ONE SAMPLE IN VARIOUS WAYS. CONSIDERATION OF THE ENTIRE COMBINATION DETERMINES THE QUALITY OF RHYTHM & FORM IN THE WRITING, AND CONSEQUENTLY THE RHYTHMIC BALANCE OF THE PERSONALITY.

CHARACTER AND PERSONALITY

DOWNSTROKES ARE THE IMMOVABLE COLUMN OF CHARACTER. THEY FORM THE SPINE OF THE LETTER AND ARE THE HEAVIER PRESSURE STROKES, AS THE CONTRACTION OF HAND MUSCLES EXPRESSES INNATE WILL POWER.

OUTWARD HORIZONTAL STROKES ARE LIGHTER IN PRESSURE. THESE ARE RELEASE STROKES SHOWING EMOTIONAL REACTION, MOVEMENT TOWARD OTHERS & INTO ENVIRONMENT.

ZONES

THE PROPORTIONS OF THE THREE ZONES DETERMINE THE BALANCE BETWEEN THE 3 BASIC AREAS OF EGO DEVELOPMENT.
UPPER ZONE: FANTASY, SPIRIT, INTELLECT
MIDDLE ZONE: SOCIAL SELF, DAILY LIFE
LOWER ZONE: INSTINCTUAL SELF...
UNCONSCIOUS DRIVES FOR SECURITY, SEX, & MATERIAL THINGS...

LINE SLOPE   WHICH SHOWS THE MOOD LEVEL...

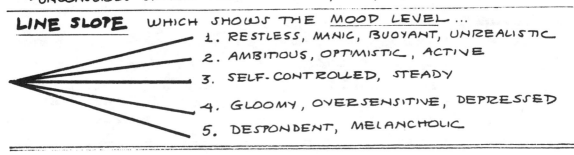

1. RESTLESS, MANIC, BUOYANT, UNREALISTIC
2. AMBITIOUS, OPTIMISTIC, ACTIVE
3. SELF-CONTROLLED, STEADY
4. GLOOMY, OVERSENSITIVE, DEPRESSED
5. DESPONDENT, MELANCHOLIC

INTRODUCTION TO HANDWRITING ANALYSIS
GRAPHOLOGY PICTOGRAPHS

ABILITY TO STAY ON THE LINE ⟋ SHOWS MORAL CONTROL..

THE <u>BASELINE</u> ACTS AS A MEDIATOR BETWEEN THE INSTINCTUAL DEMANDS OF THE LOWER ZONE, AND THE SOCIALIZED REQUIREMENTS OF THE MIDDLE ZONE, AND THE IDEALIZED EXPECTATIONS OF THE UPPER ZONE.

.. DEPENDABLE, STRAIGHTFORWARD.. *this is easy*

.. CARELESS, MOODY
MORAL CONFUSION... *well not very easy*
.. RIGID, FEAR of LOSING CONTROL.. *please be careful*

WRITING SLANT

THE <u>SLANT</u> DETERMINES THE DEGREE OF EMOTIONAL EXPRESSION AND SOCIAL DEVELOPMENT..
1. ANALYTIC, INDEPENDENT
2.⎱ EXTRAVERTED, DEMONSTRATIVE
3.⎰ SYMPATHETIC, EMOTIONAL, SENTIMENTAL
4. FANATIC, IRRESPONSIBLE, TOO EMOTIONAL
5.⎱ RESERVED, SELFISH, CAUTIOUS
6.⎰ SELF-CONSCIOUS, INNER REBELLION
7. EMOTIONAL REPRESSION, HIDING, INTROVERSION..

Reclined: A HANG-UP ON PAST EXPERIENCE PRODUCES DELAYED OR SUPERFICIAL EMOTIONAL REACTIONS..

Vertical: HEAD-OVER-HEART... OPEN TO EXPERIENCE OF THE MOMENT.. CAUTIOUS AND CONSIDERED ACTIONS..

Inclined.. IMMEDIATE REACTION TO EXPERIENCE.. DESIRE TO ACT UPON ENVIRONMENT.. GOAL ORIENTED..

Unstable.. UNPREDICTABLE REACTIONS..

PRESSURE

<u>PRESSURE</u> INDICATES THE AMOUNT of ENERGY AVAILABLE TO EGO.

pressure is symbolic   *so is lack of pressure*

ACTIVE, STRONG EGO & LIBIDO..   PASSIVE RESISTANCE.. LACK
VITAL, DURABLE, AGGRESSIVE,   OF ENERGY & LIBIDO.. VERY
FORCEFUL, ENERGETIC..   SENSITIVE, ADAPTABLE, SPIRITUAL

INTRODUCTION TO HANDWRITING ANALYSIS
GRAPHOLOGY PICTOGRAPHS

LINE THICKNESS : PASTIOSITY & SHARPNESS

fine lines .. SENSITIVE , SPIRITUAL

medium lines .. NORMAL EMOTIONAL EXPRESSION

heavy lines .. SENSUOUS, DOMINATING
MATERIALISTIC, SENTIMENTAL ..

...QUALITIES OF
SENSUALITY
& SPIRITUALITY

WRITING SIZE

.SIZE REVEALS HOW MUCH IMPORTANCE THE WRITER PLACES
UPON HIS OWN ACTIONS.

large ..INFLATED VIEW OF OWN IMPORTANCE , EXPANSIVE,
EXTROVERTED, EXTRAVAGENT, LIKES AUDIENCE.

small ..ABILITY TO CONCENTRATE & BE ALONE , MODESTY,
INTROVERTED , FRUGAL , SELF- CRITICAL ..

SPACING

SPACING REVEALS HOW CLOSE THE WRITER WISHES TO PLACE
HIMSELF TO OTHER PEOPLE OR TO SITUATIONS IN HIS EN-
VIRONMENT.   THE PAGE IS THE WRITER'S ENVIRONMENT.
THE SPACE BETWEEN THE LINES IS THE DISTANCE THE
WRITER WISHES TO KEEP FROM HIS OWN FEELINGS.
THE SPACE BETWEEN THE WORDS IS THE DISTANCE THE
WRITER SEEKS TO ESTABLISH BETWEEN HIMSELF AND
OTHERS, AND THE SPACE BETWEEN THE LETTERS SHOWS
PERSONAL EXTROVERSION OR INTROVERSION.

SPACING BETWEEN THE LINES

MUDDLED MIND	CLEAR MIND	OUT OF TOUCH
yes you will learn to think	*yes you will learn to think*	*yes you will learn to think*
CONFUSION.. NEED FOR CONTACT..	INNER BALANCE & HARMONY..	DISTRUST.. FEAR ISOLATION ..

SPACING WITHIN THE WORD

friendly EXTROVERSION; LACK of INHIBITION

cautious ..INTROVERSION, PERSONAL INHIBITION, SELF-CONSCIOUS..

SPACING BETWEEN THE WORDS

please   stay   away

NEEDS PRIVACY & DISTANCE FROM OTHERS..

be close to me

..SEEKS CONSTANT CONTACT
AND CLOSENESS..

INTRODUCTION TO HANDWRITING ANALYSIS
GRAPHOLOGY PICTOGRAPHS

SPEED

SPEED OF WRITING SHOWS MENTAL & PHYSICAL AGILITY..

a speedy script

a slow writer

VIVACIOUS, ESCAPIST, RASH,
A NATURAL PERSON, BRIGHT,
QUICK THINKER ..

CAREFUL, SLOW LOGICAL THINKER
HIDDEN FEELINGS WITH CONCERN
FOR APPEARANCES, TENSION ..

RHYTHM

RHYTHM IS DETERMINED BY THE FLOW OF THE WRITING
MOVEMENT OVER THE ENTIRE PAGE AND THE INTERPLAY
OF REPEATED AND CHANGING CHARACTERISTICS. IT IS
THE NATURAL HEARTBEAT OF HANDWRITING.

regularity of rhythm shows a balanced personality

overly rigid writing shows inhibition and fear

irregularity shows lack of personal balance + unreliability

LETTER FORM QUALITY

WRITERS CONSCIOUSLY AND UNCONSCIOUSLY DEVELOP A
PERSONAL MANNER OF FORMING LETTERS:

ORNAMENTATION .... SIMPLICITY .... NEGLECT

A Pound Of Butter
Suzi Smith

Suzi Smith
A Pound of Butter

a pound of butter
suzi smith

PROUD, FORMAL, AFFECTED
VAIN, SELF-CONSCIOUS
BAD TASTE, HIDING..

MATURE, PRACTICAL,
NATURAL & OPEN,
SPARTAN.

UNCOMMUNACATIVE
CEREBRAL, WITH-
DRAWN, DEPRESSED

LETTER SHAPES

ARCADE = RESERVE, PROTECTIVE, RESPECTS TRADITION ..

GARLAND: RECEPTIVE, ADAPTABLE, PEACE-LOVING ..

ANGLE: ENERGETIC, DECISIVE, AGGRESSIVE ..

THREAD: DIPLOMATIC, CREATIVE, QUICK MIND ..

LETTER SHAPES, WHICH INCLUDE CONNECTING STROKES, SHOW
A GENERAL PERSONALITY TYPE.

INTRODUCTION TO HANDWRITING ANALYSIS
GRAPHOLOGY PICTOGRAPHS

THE PALMER METHOD

THIS PENMANSHIP SYSTEM HAS BEEN TAUGHT IN THE MAJORITY OF AMERICAN SCHOOLS SINCE THE LATE 19th CENTURY. • THE CHARACTERS WITH THEIR EVEN SHADING, SUPERFLUOUS LEAD·INS, ENDINGS, & CURLICUES, AND SUDDEN CHANGES OF DIRECTION FORM THE COPYBOOK MODEL WHICH THE GRAPHIC ANALYST MUST REMEMBER AS A PROTOTYPE.

A B C D E F G H I J K L M N O P Q R S T U V W X Y Z

a b c d e f g h i j k l m n o p q r s t u v w x y z 1234567890

LEAD·IN AND ENDING STROKES

THESE EXTRA HAND MOVEMENTS SLOW THE MOMENTUM OF THE WRITING AND YIELD MANY PERSONALITY CLUES.

a lead·in or ending has meanings galore

CONNECTEDNESS

THE DEGREE OF CONNECTION BETWEEN THE WORDS SHOWS THE INDIVIDUAL'S INTELLECTUAL PROCESSES.

connected letters   *disconnected letters*

RELIANCE UPON LOGIC TO BUILD CAREFUL CONCLUSIONS. UNDERSTANDS SELF FIRST. RELIABLE, CONSISTENT.	RELIANCE UPON INSTINCT & INTUITION. OPEN TO OTHER'S THOUGHTS & FEELINGS. INDEPENDENT, INDIVIDUALISTIC

Three Dimensions of Movement
Zones, Slant and Pressure

All the world is but a page and each must write his part. This is the most basic principle of graphology. The writing page, as a background for the writing itself, can be considered the individual platform, stage or life-space against which the drama of life is spun out in the weavings of handwriting patterns. Taken as a whole pattern, the handwriting is a picture of how the individual fills his life-space. It is the tracing of his actions as he progresses through life, a physical expression of a mental, emotional and physical state.

We live in and move through a three-dimensional world of height, width and depth. Each of these dimensions has a symbolic correlation in graphic movement. The dimension of height, which is the vertical dimension, is seen in the proportion and movement of the letters upward and downward through the writing zones. The horizontal dimension, width, is seen in movement from left to right across the page. You will observe this sideways movement in the angle of letter slope, or slant. The third dimension, depth, is found in movement into and out of the writing surface, and is represented by force of pressure and inking patterns. The balanced individual seeks harmony between his actions and his environment. If he is successful, his writing should reflect this in good rhythm and form quality. The three dimensions of movement will integrate, and the resulting patterns will establish a harmony with the background page.

Zones: The Vertical Dimension of Movement

THE THREE ZONES OF HANDWRITING: UPPER, MIDDLE, AND LOWER

Zonal movement takes place in the vertical dimension of writing, the dimension of the self, and thus is the sturdy column of character. Zonal movement supports all of the horizontal and peripheral flourishes of personality like a backbone or a tree trunk. The proportions of the three zones determine the balance between the three major areas of ego development: the intellectual and spiritual sphere of the individual, his everyday social self and his often unconscious instinctual drives. Zonal symmetry in handwriting is a measure of the person's inner equilibrium and maturity. Symbolically the three zones can be interpreted in terms of time and space, as divisions of the body and as levels of consciousness as first defined by Sigmund Freud.

In the sequence of time, the upper zone represents the future, the middle zone the present and the lower zone the past. A spatial analogy to this would be a tree, with its branches and leaves reaching into the sky, the playground of the mind and abstract thought, its trunk thrusting out of the baseline earth, the area closest to the concerns of human endeavor, and the root system reaching unseen below representing energy in the area of instinctual drives. Good growth balance between branches, trunk and roots promises that our tree/writer will withstand many a storm.

The human body has been used in the following drawing to represent zonal areas because a person's handwriting accurately reflects the physical characteristics of each zone. The head in the upper zone (referred to as UZ, for short) contains the intellect, imagination and spiritual aspirations, as well as the articulation of the moral attitudes of the writer and his conscience. In the upper zone the writer shows the degree and quality of his self-awareness.

Physical illness or abnormalities reveal themselves as writing irregularities in the zone that corresponds to that area of the body. Upper body problems will most clearly affect the formation of the upper zone portions of letters, just as the middle zone or trunk of the body influences the flow of letter strokes in that area, and the lower zone of the writing responds to physical and psychic conditions there.

In the formation of personality the three zones interact with each other, just as the body functions as a whole. The demands of UZ rules of conduct try to adapt to the instinctual energies, unconscious drives and organic needs, which are stored in the unconscious and expressed in the lower zone (LZ) of the writing. The middle zone

8

(MZ) of handwriting embodies the ego or self-conscious, social, goal-oriented part of personality, which acts in the real world of facts, events, and other people.

Along the baseline, or morals line, of the writing can be traced the success of the balancing act between the zones. The ego is obliged to effect a smooth compromise that will satisfy both intellectual and moral considerations, as well as allow fair expression to the innate physical energies and drives welling up from the unconscious. The characteristics of the baseline indicate the degree of success the ego is having in managing these often conflicting forces in such a way as to accomplish the ego's own social and practical goals. Thus we see that handwriting, which is the mirror of the total person, cannot have one "good" zone or one "bad" zone. Here rhythmic balance is all-important for personal maturity.

UPPER ZONE = sphere of imagination, mind & spirit.. intellect & creativity..

MIDDLE ZONE = sphere of actuality.. social life.. everyday concerns

LOWER ZONE = sphere of the unconscious.. instinctual urges, material demands.. biological needs..

BASELINE

ZONAL CHARACTERISTICS

UPPER ZONE	MIDDLE ZONE	LOWER ZONE
Future	Present	Past
Upper body	Middle body	Lower body
Mental perceptions	Action	Sensual perception
Concepts	Emotional expression	Basic drives
Conscious spiritual, intellectual, and cultural aspirations	Realistic, practical and social expression of the ego	Unconscious drives and biological needs
Fantasy	Immediacy	Memory

UPPER ZONE LETTERS	MIDDLE ZONE LETTERS	LOWER ZONE LETTERS

THE ZONES IN TERMS OF GRAPHOLOGY: ZONAL BALANCE

Normal Balance Between the Zones. When the zonal dimensions are well-balanced and in good, flexible form, the writer shows stability at the most basic level, as well as involvement and initiative. He can handle his own thoughts and feelings so as to get on with others, express himself, and accomplish his goals. The ego has an inner equilibrium that accords an equal focus of attention to all areas of the writer's life.

*- mate gave me this pad
to take notes on. She's
taking a class in calligraphy
That I once took and it*

Overdevelopment of any one zone always occurs at the expense of one or both of the others. A greatly extended zone often tangles with the one above or below, which increases the confusion that the personality is having in sorting out its thoughts and drives. Sometimes illness in a portion of the body causes the corresponding zone to enlarge or distort, or both. Seen together below are examples of a single zone dominating.

DOMINANT UPPER ZONE ⋏⋏

UPPER ....
MIDDLE ....   *how I long for Los Angeles*
LOWER ...

DOMINANT MIDDLE ZONE ⋏⋏

UPPER .....
MIDDLE ....   *for my luncheon I cooked*
LOWER .....

DOMINANT LOWER ZONE ⋏⋏

UPPER ....
MIDDLE .....   *mortgage payments yield*
LOWER ....

SPECIFIC CHARACTERISTICS OF THE UPPER ZONE

Normal Upper Zone.   Graphology has made the UZ the realm of the mind and the guardian of spiritual aspirations. Here can be seen the intellect, imagination, illusion, fantasy and the drive for power. Here also, the demands of the conscience are formed, as well as an individual's idea of himself. Well-proportioned loops and stems with sensibly placed i-dots and t-bars reveal mental capability and alertness.

This season I am in the center of thousands of people. Keeps me from thinking about the family too much.

If the **Upper Zone is Overly Extended** at the expense of the MZ and the LZ, the writer will be a person of intelligence and ambition whose emotional development has not matured enough to carry out his plans with much success. Great UZ height reveals the idealist and dreamer with a wealth of theories that he cannot seem to carry through in practical experience. The tall UZ is quite literally too far away—too "far out"—to reach daily life in the MZ.

Yet a step farther from reality is the extremely tall, distorted, cracked or embellished UZ, which shows totally undirected mental activity, a retreat into fantasy that can be serious enough to indicate mental illness.

The dominant UZ also indicates the presence of a demanding conscience, one incorporating the uncompromising ideas of right and wrong learned as a child, which inhibits and depresses both the daily life and the instincts. Such a person is critical of himself and others, finds little joy in life, and under pressure flees to dreams.

the morning and pick up another couple hundred pots. We hope to have all the gear in Sunday. Monday we will load the boat and probably leave here by Tuesday.

Hope that you last a 190 first game and that 210 last watch out for the last game

When the **Upper Zone is Very Small** in relation to the MZ and LZ, the writer is one who lacks creativity and imagination; he has little capacity for and takes small pleasure in intellectual matters. His importance is placed instead upon practical considerations. In a good script he is self-reliant, realistic and sociable; with poor form level, the absence of the monitoring function of the UZ conscience leads to greed, materialism and sensuality.

Since the UZ is the origin of conceptual self-orientation and much of a person's self-awareness, when this zone is stunted, the writer is likely to lack understanding of his goals, his self-image or the impression he wishes to make.

Once upon a time there were three little bears, mama bear, papa bear, baby bear

Widely Inflated or Swollen UZ loops are a sign of overcompensation for feelings of intellectual inferiority and an emotional need for constant reassurance. The bloated UZ loop writer resorts to exaggeration and boastfulness to compensate for his low opinion of himself. His boasts, of course, are based on fantasy.

a good buy" spouse would have option of the proceeds — lum sum or monthly — while 2nd career

Stick Figure UZ Formations indicate a realistic, practical, and independent thinker, one with a controlled but inquiring mentality that thrives on facts. Indeed, such a person is most at home with concrete data; he mistrusts mental embroidery and subjective thinking.

Now is the time for all good men to come to the aid of the Party.

Retraced UZ Formations always show inhibition and repression in the intellectual life. When the hand moves back along the same stroke so that the result is one line where there would normally be a loop, the graphological meaning is the inhibition of feeling because of painful associations. Because loops represent emotion, the retraced writer is denying much of his creative and intellectual stimulus and capacity. The realm of spirit and ideas has associations with ridicule or failure for him.

It was a shame that the weather was miserable today. It would have been nice for the out-of-towners

Thrusts into the UZ. A thrust is a sudden plunge of the pen from one zone of handwriting into another; it is legible and does not cross into other letter strokes. Thrusts upward indicate one who uses a keen mind to advantage, a person who is constantly thinking in a creative and innovative way, actively using his mental talents.

When too many of these MZ forms thrust themselves into the UZ, the writing betrays a brilliant mind that is determined to show off its cleverness. Such writers are often successful authors, actors or musicians, but they always need an audience.

Though no replies, my mind tells me to keep reminding you to write or at least not forget our discussions

Tangling. A tangled UZ is one that runs into the line above it in a random and messy manner. Tangling most frequently appears in the LZ because that portion of writing fluctuates and enlarges most easily; it is not often seen in the upper or middle zones. Tangling between zones always shows distraction in that area of life, sometimes to the point of irresponsibility. In the UZ the interpretation is muddled thinking, mental clutter and jumble of unsorted stimuli, thought and reactions. Such writers often have, however, surprising charm and creativity.

'3, newly married also to a very pretty pleasant young lady. — All

Points at the Top of Loops are clues to a person of intelligence who thinks of himself as being different from others, of marching to a different drum. Sometimes he feels isolated and lonely and other times thinks himself in possession of special truths and insights. He is prone to emotional thinking and usually has feelings against established ideas or authority.

and am looking forward to it so much. It is nice to be here at Gary's home for the first time. It is charming.

Little Balloons as UZ Loops, particularly with a swingling lead-in, are a sure sign of originality of thought and a sense of humor. These little round areas must be close to the MZ and natural-looking, not isolated embellishments at the end of a long stick, which would indicate eccentricity.

That money talks I'll not deny. I heard it once, It said goodbye.

SPECIFIC CHARACTERISTICS OF THE MIDDLE ZONE

Normal Middle Zone. What the writer thinks of himself and of his role in life, and how he can be expected to project this self-image onto others is expressed in the MZ. This area reveals the quality and consistency of effort toward the conscious pursuit of goals. MZ emphasis is upon social and work activity and shows the individual's actual progression into the environment. Medium height, in balance with the other zones, and well-formed letters indicate wholesome self-confidence and sensible adjustment to life.

Mike and Barbara stopped over for a cup of coffee last night.

If the **Middle Zone is Strongly Developed,** but neither the upper nor lower zones are, the writer is one who is overly concerned for himself and his own daily activities. His self-assurance borders on presumptuousness and conceit, and he will make great issues of trivial things. The danger to this sort of writer is boredom and confinement in a self-centered world. The degree of fluctuation in middle zone letter size and disconnectedness are indicators of the sensitivity of the person to feeling and experience.

The low super-ego or conscience development in very large MZ writers leads to difficulty in delaying pleasure. Often leaders, self-reliant, strong-willed, and practical where letters are clearly formed, these writers cannot achieve a harmonious realism within themselves because they lack mature detachment and philosophical attitudes.

A very small writing can be entirely of MZ emphasis with no extensions into the UZ or LZ. In this case, the smaller and more uniform the letter size, the more compulsive and perfectionistic the writer.

of the "to be returned" items. Hope Jook's letter arrives in time. Dapper

If the **Middle Zone is Dwarfed** by the UZ and LZ, the person tends to underrate himself and suffer from inferiority feelings; he finds little joy in daily life and prefers not to cope with its problems. In studying the zones, however, notice how good a balancing act the MZ, or ego, is maintaining. If the MZ is very small but both of the other zones are extended and the baseline firm but flexible, the personality has found equilibrium, albeit on a tightrope. With good form quality, such a writer is usually creative.

Writing is never fun for me but it is fun to see if my personality is changing any. The probability exists that am is together and I'm apart. But we'll have t

A Very Small MZ in writing with all the zones well-formed and in proportion, shows a writer of great independence who can shut out ego needs and concentrate long hours alone. With original characteristics and form level, these writers are geniuses. One such writer was Albert Einstein, whose writing appears on page 92.

visiting my friend on Bainbridge Island (Puget Sound) and with another friend on Orcas Island in the San Juans. So enjoyed the time there and especially the cool weather, the green forests and the water. We were also two days on the coast/

Fluctuation in MZ Letter Size is the key to determining mood stability. A combination of large and small letters in the same word and line warns of emotional volatility. Such moodiness and inconsistency of reaction makes the person hard to understand and get along with. Excessive fluctuation in *any* zone points to great impressionability and difficulty in coping with emotional stimuli.

said I could be her helper, which means, I get to stay after school, and clean the erasers. That's all I have

Jerks and Breaks in MZ Letters. A break in a letter occurs when the hand interrupts its movement just enough to leave the slightest opening in the stroke that forms the letter, not the connecting stroke. These breaks, and also jerks and tremors, are the result of anxiety and tension. Fears, work pressure, a strong inner judgmental system, a personal problem, any such tensions can unconsciously inhibit and cramp body muscles long enough to affect the flow of the writing.

Now is the time for all good men to

Tangling in the MZ shows in the snarling, coiling and overlapping of strokes in this ego area. Here is someone who takes on more than he can handle; he is impractical and cannot manage his work in an orderly way. His social goals, duties, and obligations are similarly confused and undisciplined. The writer will have the warmth and sociability that goes with loopy strokes, but the potential for dishonesty is great.

Nothing wrong with the World only the people in it.

The tangling in the signature of the famous musician above shows difficulty in handling everyday affairs as they relate to the public image. It also illustrates the freedom and creativity of a gifted artist.

BASELINES

The baseline of a handwriting forms an invisible line between the middle and upper zones above and the lower zone below. Through its characteristics of levelness or unsteadiness it shows how well the personality is handling the mixture of influences from the intellectual, social and instinctual drives.

Visualize the baseline as a linear graph between the ego and the conscience above and somatic tensions below; if it holds steady but relaxed, the writing is closer to a healthy whole, but if it is tugged up by thoughts and ego concerns and down by instinctual needs, or if it is as rigid as a bayonet, the personality is in trouble. As an indicator of mood, moral and social control, temperament, disposition and flexibility, the baseline is the ego-adjustment line.

NORMALLY STRAIGHT LINES: Composure, orderliness, emotional stability, dependability, perseverance.

The writer's mind disciplines his emotions.

. - U. women in particular .
Daly at the U. U. A. General
New York in 1974, where she
enthusiastic packed auditorium,

RIGID: Overcontrol for fear of losing control, inhibited.

The writer protects himself against additional outbursts, but drains his spontaneity and energy for action.

plans too much. Unless I drop
dead I will leave here Friday
morning and be there as soon as

ERRATIC: Unstable moods and working habits, indecisiveness, confusion between reality and illusion, hyper-emotional, lacking in will-power.

SINUOUS: Flexible, nervous, energetic, diplomatic, sometimes exciteable and moody.

The writer's moral values are flexible; he is very responsive to the influences of others.

RISING: Buoyant spirit, ambition, optimism, restlessness.

The writer wants to escape the demands of routine. He is excitable and quickly stirred to action. At times he loses himself to external influences.

SPECIFIC WORDS RISE: Indicates positive emphasis on that particular word.

FALLING: Fatigue, depressions, disappointment, unhappiness, discouragement. Also, obstinacy and determination.

The writer has difficulty in giving up his self concepts for others.

SPECIFIC WORDS FALL: Indicates negative or uneasy feeling about that particular word.

HOLLOW or CONCAVE LINES: Starts enthusiastically, then loses interest, but musters energy to finish.

ARCHED or CONVEX LINES: Ambitions and enthusiasm but too little stamina or energy to sustain interest.

I really want to play the violin like you want me to

DESCENDING STEPS: Writer fights against depressive mood.

With just a little more effort I can finish

ASCENDING STEPS: Writer must continually check his impulse to become overly optimistic or excited.

The lawsuit was filed in Court and I am quite certain to win.

SPECIFIC CHARACTERISTICS OF THE LOWER ZONE

Normal Lower Zone.   The LZ is below the level of consciousness. Inborn biological drives, instinctual urges for security and satisfaction, and material demands jostle here with unacknowledged memories and experiences from the first hours of life. In our culture this powerful realm of drives and sensations is the most private. A normal LZ is usually slightly longer than the UZ, and there is the possibility for more variety of form here within the bounds of legibility and good rhythm. Look for smoothly written, unembellished strokes of a size that balances with the other zones.

We're looking forward to a great evening tonight and anxious to know what you're going to tell me about my handwriting —

If the **LZ Dominates** in size both the middle and upper zones, it follows that the writer will be dominated by those powerful unconscious forces relating to survival needs, materialism and reproductive imperatives. Driven excessively by instinctual wants, the large, loopy LZ writer is restless and needs constant variety and change; much of his time is spent trying to satisfy his enormous appetites for money, sex and variety. When his security needs take over, this person exhibits a neurotic infantilism, a purposeful lack of control over his daily life. Such emotional people have creative ideas and physical energy, but need help in carrying out a project.

I am enjoying this party very much.

The smoke however, is not so enjoyable.

Tangling easily occurs with large and exaggerated lower loops. This adds further psychic confusion. Now the person has trouble determining just which of his instinctual needs is pressuring him, and becomes inwardly too disordered to satisfy any of them. Also, a physical illness that makes more demands than the patient can handle will cause the lower zone to balloon or distort.

I am enjoying the most interesting guests who are all having a grand time. I do hope that; you

A **Stunted Lower Zone** in proportion to the upper and middle zones expresses a lack of the material rootedness and concern necessary for successful planning in life, or can indicate sexual immaturity, fear or trauma.

Roses are Red yellow Pink and white, but they're not in Calif. for years.

Sincerely

Retraced LZ. The introduction of material from the unconscious mind into consciousness can be painful, particularly early childhood traumas and sexual feelings that were learned as "bad." One defense is repression of these hurts, keeping them unconscious, where they remain unacknowledged, a source of tension and loss of energy to the ego. This repression shows in retraced LZ strokes; instead of a loop or a straight downstroke, the hand carefully comes back up over the downstroke, covering it and canceling it out. These writers have blocked so much responsiveness that close relationships with them are difficult.

Be sure to call when youre in New york —

Short Stick Figure Lower Zone writers can be counted upon to be practical and independent. This type of self-directed writer is determined not to become caught up in the needs and emotional powers of the LZ. When the short downward stroke ends in a pool of ink, the expression of physical or sexual energy has become blunted too soon, however, and the extra aggressive force is capable of expressing itself in a negative way. In low-quality writings these endings are called "clubs," and they show a capacity for cruelty.

When the downstroke is long but ends in a pool of ink, it means that the person has energy left over and is capable of continued determination.

Dad told me that if you marry for money you will earn every penny of it. An hour ceremony starts a lifetime of trouble, he says.

Long Stick Figures in the LZ share the hesitancy of the short stick figure writer to become emotionally engaged in LZ considerations, but the additional length here means restlessness and above all, defensiveness. This writer feels very vulnerable and fears actually losing himself to his drives or to others with strong instinctual demands. He draws a wall to protect himself. If the stroke ends in a point, he is all the more sensitive and vulnerable to others' basic demands.

Triangles in the LZ are slow and awkward for the hand to write; all hesitancy carries a strong meaning. In women's writings LZ triangles show prudishness and a strongly judgmental nature regarding sexual matters. Triangles in a male LZ are evidence of the "Virgin Mary Complex." Often a religious upbringing or bias leads the man to think of sex as unclean and a woman with whom he enjoys sex as "bad." He will marry or admire the good, clean woman but inevitably find real sexual satisfaction only with a prostitute, or a woman he is not obliged to respect.

Great Variety in LZ Forms.   Harmonious variety in handwritten forms is always a plus. But excessive changes and flip-flops in any zone show internal personality conflict; in the LZ this takes the form of unsettled sexual focus. While it is not possible to determine gender from handwriting, nor, with any consistency, sexual preference, a confused or bisexual personality is always evident in writing with three or four noticeably different LZ formations.

JERRY LEWIS
Actor.

DOUGLAS FAIRBANKS,
Actor.

I never knew but one man who could. I knew he could, however, because he told me so himself. He was a middle-aged, simple-hearted miner who had lived

MARK TWAIN, Author.

COLETTE, Author.

I walking on the street to get the horse and that is all

Valentina

VALENTINA, Clothes designer.

Thank you for the book. I should have written for but burnt Smith for a few do and forgot other things

GEORGIA O'KEEFE, Artist.

Once again you've come through
victorious + practically unscathed
through the barrage

BILL HAYES, Actor.

and self-respect exists for every man, however handicapped; but that niche must be found for him. To carry the process of restoration to a point short of this is to leave the Cathedral without a Spire.

John Galsworthy

JOHN GALSWORTHY,
Author.

Now is the time for all good men
to come to the aid of this party.

Pete Seeger

PETE SEEGER,
Musician.

Arthur Knight

ARTHUR KNIGHT,
Film critic.

Well Here's everything
you wish yourself on Christmas

Ronald Reagan

RONALD REAGAN, Politician.

Kate Smith.

KATE SMITH,
Musician.

sempre memore tuo
e riconoscente ...

caro signor Jules Dufour

... Ang. Ben. con, sincere
... fervore

POPE JOHN XIII
Ecclesiastic.

HENRY CABOT LODGE
Politician.

RED SKELTON
Comedian.

I am going down
the street to get the
Horse and carriage out
of the Garage

HEDY LAMARR, Actress.

With appreciation
for all your help —

ROMMEL
German general.

TED KENNEDY, Politician.

... through residence on Wall
... who says that "Sitting still
... is the heavenly way, the going
... the way of the world." Yet
... evaporation, and by a thousand

HENRY THOREAU, Author.

25

Slant: The Horizontal Dimension of Movement

Whenever you write, you are expressing your present situation, so that all writing is an instantaneous graph of that exact moment. But writing is also a sequential movement that takes place through time. The beginning of a message is older than its end. The beginning of a line at the left of a page is older than the end of that same line at the right. As you move away from the left side of the page, you are beginning. You are moving away from your past. As you progress to the right, you are moving toward your goal, completion.

The left of the page, left of a word, the beginning stroke—these are all placements in the past. Alternately, the right of the page, the right of a word and the ending strokes are all directions to the future. It can be seen that this left/right movement through time takes place along the baseline in the horizontal dimension. Since the baseline has already been identified in meaning with the surface of the earth, action along it implies contact with environment. Horizontal movement is a measure of external orientation and social development. Here you can observe the manner in which the writer faces life situations, his abilities to communicate and express himself emotionally, his choices of behavior and his objectives. Along this horizontal plane, all of these aspects of personality are clearly revealed.

The angle of slant observed in a writing will tell you more about the nature of the writer's personality than any other consideration of horizontal movement. It is extremely important to recognize the differences between what an appraisal of zones tells you about the writer's *inner* character, and what slant tells you about his *outer* personality.

ZONES AND THE VERTICAL DIMENSION	SLANT AND THE HORIZONTAL DIMENSION
Character	Personality
Self	Others
Perception	Emotion
Internal	External
Containment	Dispersement
Perception	Reaction
Analysis	Relationship
Thought	Communication
Individual	Social

HOW TO MEASURE SLANT

The slant of a writing refers to the direction of letter slope and is determined by the angle formed between the downstroke and the baseline.

Measure upper and middle zone letters to determine slant. Whenever possible, use stick figures, as they are less confusing than loops. With loopy writing, take an average of the loop by measuring from the apex at the highest point of the letter to where the lines cross near the baseline. Downstrokes will give you a more accurate measurement than upstrokes.

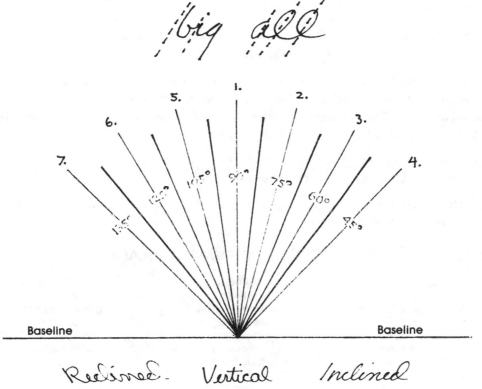

Place the slant graph over or near the writing sample you wish to measure. Locate the angle of slant that most closely approximates that of the sample. Remember to keep the baseline of the graph parallel to and on top of the baseline of the sample. The point of the arrow should be on the baseline at the base of the letter you wish to measure. Measure several upper and middle zone letters, note the corresponding numbers, and then check your measurement on the expanded graph.

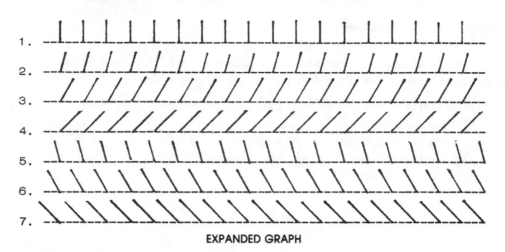

1.
2.
3.
4.
5.
6.
7.

EXPANDED GRAPH

A variation between two positions on the slant chart is considered a normal degree of fluctuation. With a variation of more than two positions, the slant is considered unstable. The more extreme the degree of variation, the more unstable is the emotional and social expression of the writer.

When the slant never varies at all, it can be determined that there is some emotional rigidity being expressed by the writer.

After some practice measuring slant with the graph, you will be able to determine slant with just your eye.

SOME KEY WORDS ASSOCIATED WITH VARIOUS SLANTS

RECLINED	VERTICAL	INCLINED
past	present	future
influence of mother	independence	goals of father
fear	inner strength	courage
defiance	self-reliance	compliance
introversion	self-control	extroversion
lack of involvement	judgment	compassion
repression	suppression	expression
self-absorption	independence	drawn to others
caution	action	reaction

*Observe that the vertical slant has many traits in common with zones and the vertical dimension in general.

SPECIFIC CHARACTERISTICS OF SLANT

1. Vertical.   This type has a head-over-heart emotional attitude. He is open to the experience of the moment, but his responses are cautious and considered. Here emotional expression is under control. The manner is undemonstrative, independent, detached and even indifferent. Once emotional control is lost it is quickly regained, hence this type functions well in emergencies and makes a good leader or contented loner. The person is self-interested and asks, "What can the situation do for me?'' In arguing a point, this writer will make an appeal to judgment rather than to emotion. Often he has a great deal of personal magnetism and a dry wit that is quite attractive.

Outside of the prune-industry press, I've seen very little copy on our show during the past few months.

2. Inclined. This slant is considered the ''normal'' one. The writer is normally sensitive and emotionally healthy, but modest with responses. Judgment and logic rule, yet more sympathy and compassion are expressed here than in the vertical slant. The range of expression is seldom over-demonstrative.

To thine own self be true and it shall follow as the night the day ——.

3. Very Inclined. These people cry and laugh readily, give vent to their feelings, are future- and goal-oriented and have an ardent, affectionate, amiable and sensitive emotional nature. They express their emotional self impulsively. Feelings will influence decisions, and they are quick to react with elation or discouragement. They identify with their surroundings and with another person's point of view and will respond with compassion.

Its fleece was white as snow and everywhere that Mary went the lamb was sure to go.

4. Extremely Inclined. This type is a volcano of emotional reactions: extremely ardent, passionate, jealous, easily offended, very demonstrative with affections, susceptible to hurt and can hate bitterly and with abandon, loves the same way, restless, unsettled, impulsive, capable of hysteria, wears self out, strongly influenced by likes and dislikes, can be stirred by and stirs other peoples' emotions, plunges into relationships or causes; an emotional brushfire.

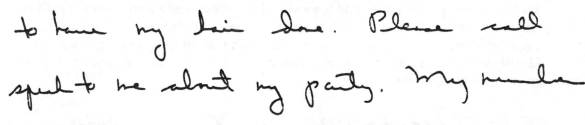

The more the writing leans to the right past #4, the more extreme the social and emotional behavior. This is very abnormal, and a strong indication of fanaticism and emotional illness.

5. Reclined. The public self-image of the reclined writer is often quite polished. Don't be fooled. It's a well constructed front made to cover up and compensate for inner withdrawal. These writers somehow manage to be charming in social situations while remaining emotionally aloof. Feelings are repressed—fears and anxieties are not acknowledged. These writers are out of touch with themselves emotionally yet are self-absorbed at the same time. They feel an inward longing to be different and will give more to the development of inner abilities and resources than to emotional development. Often there is found an immature attachment to the ideals and values of their mother figure, who has usually played the dominant role in shaping the social personality. In most cases of reclined writing, the father has played a weak or negative role, and positive male identification is jeopardized. Reclined writers resist accepting progress or change.

6. Very Reclined. This type of slant indicates complete self-interest. The writer is independent, hard to fathom and difficult to get along with. He may act friendly while keeping you at arms' length but rarely shows true feelings or desires. He is past-oriented and strongly influenced by the values of his mother. Emotionally, he is cold, yet may still seem sociable.

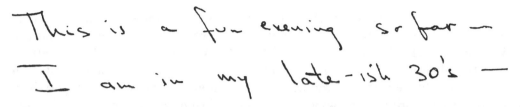

7. Extremely Reclined.

This slant is very rare. This type has all of the above characteristics amplified. The behavior is very evasive and the emotional nature is withdrawn. The writer is out of touch with his environment and lives in the past. Mother identification is so strong that individual development is blocked. These writers can still show the well-developed and charming public personality so often found with the reclined slant.

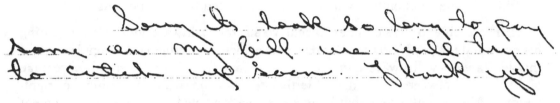

8. Unstable Slant.

This type is unsettled and inconsistent. He is subject to the moods and thoughts of the moment. The emotional nature is erratic; you never know how he will react. He swings between repression and expression with a complete lack of prevailing attitude. The nature is nervous, undisciplined, capricious, excitable, fickle and lacking in good judgment or common sense. Inside, the person feels socially inferior and off-center.

A CONSIDERATION OF THE EFFECTS OF HANDEDNESS ON SLANT

When a righthanded person swings that arm away from the body, it swings out in a righthand direction. This is the direction of contact with environment. In writing, the natural swing of the hand produces a slant of 35 to 40 degrees rightward. If one is righthanded yet slants to the left, it is a sign of contact avoidance and concentration instead upon the self.

But what about lefthanders? Research has shown that they have an impulse to swing the left arm away from the body in a leftward direction. The most natural writing for a lefthander would be from right to left with reversed letter formations and a leftward slope of 35 to 40 degrees. In order to conform to the writing style of the western world, he must continually fight the impulse to go to the left, and must come up with a more natural way of producing a rightward slant and direction. Some lefthanded writings reveal the frustration of their counter-movements while others do not. Why is this so?

Physically, the angle of slant comes about as a result of body positioning. The pen to the fingers and hand, the hand to the writing surface, the angle of that surface to the writers body—all are important factors. But body position is only the means of achieving the slant on life which has been dictated by the emotions.

It is possible for a lefthander to achieve a fluid, rightward motion by adjusting his body and the paper, so there is very little evidence to support the popular notion that lefthanders will always slant to the left. In fact, there is only a small percentage of difference between the number of lefthanders who do so and the number of right-handers. This is not to deny that handedness plays a role in the social development of an individual. There is evidence that it does. Yet in the final analysis, we must assume that when a writer is allowed to adjust his body position to the pen and writing surface, he will, regardless of handedness, produce the slant that correctly describes his ability to express himself socially.

SLANT SPECIFICS

When I first began I was much more shy.	Person begins with reserve, then drops it and proceeds normally forward.
This time he made me feel so much	Begins with control but then quickly gets carried away.
Was great at the start but then soon	Starts off with enthusiasm, then gets more controlled.
I felt so happy	Sudden change of slant on one word indicates discomfort with the word—could be a lie.
My lover is just great.	Repressive feelings are associated with this word.
My lover is just great	Expressive feelings associated with this word.

The Reclined "I". Some writers manage to remain consistent in their angle of slant except for the personal pronoun "I." This is an indication of repression regarding the self-image. These people are better at understanding everyone else's problems than their own. They have a fixation on the mother figure which blocks the avenue to emotional maturity.

Today was a very hectic day for me. I started out looking for apartments. I found a very nice apartment but I can't seem to make up my

Lower Zones that Pull to the Right. In this example the lower zone has taken a reclined position. This is an indication of repression of instinctual needs and feelings. Sexual energy has been displaced into work or other goal-directed pursuits.

I'm glad you finally got back — & that things are at least going smoothly here! The weather especially

It is certainly good to hear from you. It has been too long! Hope all is going well and that you have completely recovered. Illness is no fun.

The example above clearly illustrates both the reclined "I" and rightward pulling lower zones.

Lower Zones that Pull to the Left. This indicates dependence on others for fulfillment of inner needs and drives. Men with this type of lower zone slant change are dependent on their wives or lovers and feel shattered by any breakup of that relationship. They often marry young and will quickly remarry if the first union ends. In this case the wife or partner is seen as an extension of the mother/son relationship. Women with this type of lower zone are also very dependent on their spouses. They continue to seek the security of childhood through their mates and expect a form of mothering from them. Both sexes seem fixated on a need for maternal care.

for some reason, maybe just to wish you a happy day.

Spending more money these days

people happy

with government

Thank you for writing to me. It's fun living in the White House, and I'm glad you are my friend.

Amy Carter

AMY CARTER, Daughter of President Jimmy Carter.

Jerry

EDMOND G. BROWN, JR. (JERRY), California Governor.

In a long and wandering life, some resentful have forced themselves on me. Perhaps those among any readers who have vagrant blood will find echoes of experience in a few generations.

JOHN STEINBECK, Writer.

What do you think of my handwriting sample today

Dennis Weaver

DENNIS WEAVER, Actor.

PATRICIA HEARST Kidnapped heiress.

We had to smash the dependencies created by monogomous sexual relationships, and to do this we had to destroy monogomy in the cell. Monogomy only serves to reinforce male supremacy and the oppression of women. Monogomy means that "the men wear the pants."

We had to destroy all the attitudes that make people think that they have to be monogomous; fear and passivity, false sense of security, power-trips,

for her tribute to me on her show. Most rewarding of all was the Enthusiasm I felt that I was the recipient of the 5th Life Achievement award. *Bette Davis*

prompted you to write me, & only hope my performances may continue to please!

Sincerely
Bette Davis

BETTE DAVIS,
Actress,
Two samples
expressing different
moods.

Evelyn and I feel a deep appreciation and gratefulness toward you for your faithful fellowship in the ministry of Christ which we share.

ORAL ROBERTS,
Religious leader.

This is my story both humble and true Take it to pieces and mend it with glue.

John Lennon 1969 Feb.

JOHN LENNON, Musician,
one of the Beatles.

JULIAN BOND, Georgian
Congressman.

ROBERT LOUIS
STEVENSON,
Poet.

This be the verse you grave for me:
Here he lies where he longed to be;
Home is the sailor, home from sea,
And the hunter home from the hill

O pretty Maiden with golden hair,
Brighter than ever my feathers were;
When you and your lover meet to-day,
You will thank me for looking some other way!

Henry W. Longfellow.

HENRY WADSWORTH LONGFELLOW, Writer.

Would like to drop in and see you —
You have a wonderful car. Been driving
it for three weeks. Its a treat to drive one
Your Slogan should be.
Drive a Ford and watch the other cars
fall behind you. I can make any other
in take a Fords dust
Bye — Bye.
John Dillinger

JOHN DILLINGER,
Bank robber and murderer.

To step out now
would be wrong for
your country, and B

LADY BIRD JOHNSON,
Wife of President
Lyndon Johnson.

CAROL BURNETT,
Entertainer.

What do you think of my
handwriting sample today?

Carol Burnett Hamilton

Sweet did she smile and graceful did she move
My blue eyed Adele, my first dear love!
I thought that day my life I would resign
When Addy took another name than mine.
Go to! I live my folly to disown
And my dear Adele weighs eighteen stone.

WILLIAM THACKERAY, Writer.

Pressure: The Depth Dimension of Movement

Pressure is the degree of force applied by the writer against the writing surface. It is also the resultant thinness or thickness of the stroke and the relative pastiosity or sharpness of the inking pattern.

THE DEGREE OF FORCE

The force of the pressure tells you how much energy is available for work or for goal-directed pursuits. Think of pressure as outward-pouring energy meeting the resistance of the environment. The energy pouring outward is the life force of the ego as seen in the writing stroke. The resistance is everyone and everything else the ego encounters, and is symbolized by the writing surface.

The degree of force can only be determined by feeling an original sample with your thumb and index finger. After you have felt a lot of samples, you will begin to know when a writing is unusually heavy or unusually light in pressure. Your eye can aid you, but the eye is better at determining the thinness or thickness of the stroke or the relative pastiosity and sharpness of the inking pattern—the other two aspects of pressure. It is very difficult to assess the force of pressure from photocopies.

Upstrokes are release strokes and are indicated by dotted lines. Downstrokes are contracting strokes and are indicated by solid lines.

The contraction and release action of the fingers continually modifies the force of the pen against the paper. It is natural for the upstrokes and the rightward strokes (release) to be somewhat lighter than the downstrokes (contraction). Contracting strokes carry more strength. This can be demonstrated by the jaw or the hand. When you clench your jaw or your fist, more strength is exerted than is possible by opening your jaw or extending your fingers.

It is important to observe how the strength of pressure is maintained as the direction of the stroke changes. This determines how the writer is able to project his available energy upon his environment.

We all had a good laugh

Pressure strong on directional change indicates that the energy level is consistent yet flexible.

and wonderful gift

Pressure weak on directional change shows an inability to modify actions in time to meet environmental changes smoothly.

Heavy Pressure.   These types make an impression. There is a great deal of energy available to them for their actions. They express in a heavy manner, are strong-willed, firm and easily excited to hot-blooded actions. Those with forceful pressure can inspire others. Negatively, they can be stern, stubborn and inclined to morose thoughts or depression. You definitely know when they are around.

Is there a problem here?

Extremely Heavy.   This person falls into a category of reversal of the usual meaning of heavy pressure. He cannot seem to release the forces within to meet the environment and overcome its resistance. This type is internally inhibited, and his power is blocked from expression.

When extreme pressure is found in the vertical dimension (up and down movement) the writer adheres strongly to his principles. He is proud, even boastful, and self-reliant rather than trusting of others. He is tenacious, fearful of change, self-centered and possibly even brutal. Expect intense sexual preoccupation from this writer as over-compensation for feelings of sexual inadequacy and inhibition. Sometimes libertine behavior develops or the sexual energy is displaced and the writer is overly ambitious. He is critical, irritable and opinionated.

Did not feel that

Today is Thursday, and what a nice visit we've had, eh? Let me know how you

When extreme pressure is found in the horizontal dimension (lead-in, ending and connecting strokes or t-bars) the person feels a split between his inner vitality and his ability to express it. The social self, the personality, will express erratically and often flamboyantly, sometimes striking out with vocal tirades or physical movements. Remember that it isn't natural to be heavy on these release strokes. This is one sign of the schizoid personality and is also seen in the writing of highly-anxious or hysterical types.

Sudden bursts of pressure within a generally heavy pattern are displayed in the writing of the paranoid personality. The paranoid is unable to take responsibility for the hostility he feels inside, and instead sees it reflected back at him from others.

Pressure exerted at the top of a letter instead of increasing with the downward motion can be taken as another sign of anxiety.

Remember that the above specific characteristics of pressure must be seen in combination with very heavy pressure in order to interpret the misplaced pressure pattern as extreme.

Medium Pressure.   This is the norm between the extremes and is an indication of healthy vitality and willpower.

Light Pressure. These people possess a certain delicacy of feeling. The personality is sensitive and impressionable. There is often great creative ability, but the potential is seldom fulfilled as these writers seem unable to absorb their experiences. The willpower is not strong, so the light-pressure writer can easily succumb to the dominance of a heavier writer. They are far more tolerant and genial than their counterparts, and though they can lapse into superficiality, their lack of inhibition can be refreshing. When the rest of the writing is harmonious, the finest peaks of spirituality and idealism are reached.

I've never known a happily married woman who wasn't having an affair

With unharmonious writing, light pressure is an indicator of fragility and weak nerves.

At an extreme point of lightness within the pressure pattern we reach the same reversal of meaning we do with very heavy pressure. It takes a certain amount of strength and willpower to check pressure. This passive resistance is expressed gently, but is a firm indication of a refusal to be committed. Very light pressure frequently turns up in the writing of actors or actresses, who must be able to drop their own force of personality in order to play the role of another.

How do I love thee?
Let me count the ways

THE WIDTH OF THE STROKE

The relative thinness or thickness of the stroke tells us how the writer displays energy in action. This aspect of pressure has more to do with the manner in which a person grasps the pen than it does with muscular energy.

One pen can produce different results in the hands of different people. The following three examples were supplied by three different individuals using the same pen—a wide-point felt tip. Note the unique effect produced by each writer.

How can you tell me
I am neither frustrated nor
neurotic — only empathetic.

The party is lovely

It is also true that the choice of the pen or pencil plays an important part in this assessment. One person can produce different widths with different pens. The following five examples were penned by one individual using various instruments. It becomes obvious that the pen plays a role in the resultant thickness of the stroke.

1. Shall I compare thee to a summer's day?

2. Thou art more lovely and more temperate.

3. Rough winds do shake the darling buds of May,

4. And summer's lease hath all too short a date:

5. Sometime too hot the eye of heaven shines,

    1. Broad-tip felt tip   2. Fine-line ball point   3. Medium-soft pencil
    4. Soft pencil   5. Fine-line felt tip

The person who chooses a pen or pencil that traces a thick line is stating a preference for a thick stroke. Likewise, one who chooses a pen which draws a thin line has a preference for this thinner stroke.

Four Widths of Stroke

Standard. How do you recognize the standard width? As you study the sample you note that the strokes maintain an equality with the background of the page—they aren't thick or thin. These types can be said to possess discipline, but without the creativity of either of the extremes. Their energy is displayed conservatively through conventional means.

Have a good time shopping in Hong Kong
and Bangkok. Will be looking
forward to your homecoming in good

Thick. These strokes are soft and dark and appear to dominate the background of the page. They are made by those who apply their energy to everything they do. These writers have a vitality about them and seek a wide range of application for their energies. They become so involved in whatever they are doing that future obligations can be momentarily forgotten. They are sentimental in nature and express it warmly.

There will be some stories coming up in the L.A. Times (maybe mentioning me) — plus Time + Newsweek this week (not

Thin. These strokes appear dry and sparse on the background of the page. Those who write with thin strokes are attentive to detail and concept. They are intellectual in their approach to life. They apply their energy with precision and efficiency.

Four score and seven years ago I was born on this grand earth. How long I shall remain I know not. But who cares? Do you, or you; or even you? I

Shaded (Thick and Thin). Writing on a page is marked by two dimensions, height and width. Pressure with shading produces the third dimension, depth. When generally heavy pressure is accompanied by shading of the stroke, it is the mark of creativity. These writers respond sensually to color, light and sound in the environment. Artists of all kinds, as well as individuals who are creative in their work, are to be found within this group. The shading of the stroke can be seen in both vertical and horizontal movement.

my guitar died one day this spring. this made me very sad. as we were becoming the closest

In this example, the broad-point of the pen nib makes the shading easy to observe.

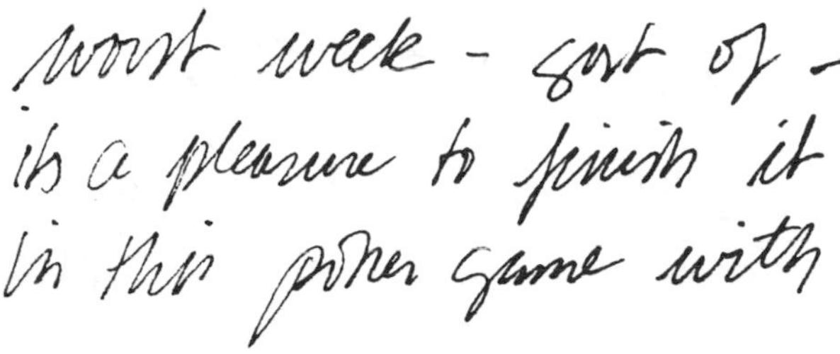

[handwritten sample, left]

This example is also shaded. In this case, the fine-line felt tip makes it more difficult to spot.

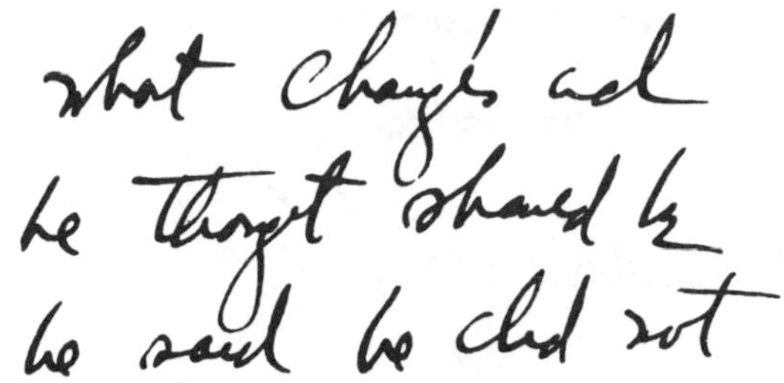

[handwritten sample, right]

This sample was penned with a fountain pen. It is easy to see the shading of the stroke.

PASTIOSITY

The word "pastiose" describes a stroke that is thick and doughy looking. It results from the relaxed manipulation of the pen, which allows for more ink flow. The manner in which the arm rests on the writing surface helps determine this, as does the pause before the change in direction of the stroke. Writing records these nearly imperceptible changes in the flow of the ink, as even a slight pause allows more ink to spill from the pen to produce an extra dark spot. Generally, sharper strokes are faster ones, while the blur of pastiosity indicates a slowing down.

To understand this better, think of the writing as a roadway mapped out by the path of an automobile. As the car approaches the turn, it slows to a degree dependent on the abruptness of the turn and then accelerates as it makes the turn. This slowing and speeding up helps the car (and the writing stroke) maintain a smooth traction on the roadway (the paper). To detect pastiosity, look for a blob of ink or a slight widening of the strokes near the tops of upper zone and the bottoms of lower zone loops at the completion of curves. Often the blob will be followed by a slight lightening of the stroke. Do not confuse these blobs of pastiosity with "dotting." Pastiosity occurs on the stroke and is part of it. For dotting to occur, the pen must actually lift from the paper and set down again. Thus it may be seen anywhere in the writing—either alongside or on top of the stroke.

Much apparent pastiosity is the result of a broken-down pen. Some ballpoints spill indiscriminantly, and some fountain pens or felt-tip pens have damaged points. Careful consideration of the sample should enable you to distinguish pen failure from extreme pastiosity.

The relative pastiosity or sharpness of the inking pattern will tell you how sensual or spiritual the writer is.

Normal Pastiosity. These writers have normal sensual and emotional responses; there is a desire for tactile stimulation and the need for physical contact with others. Another interpretation of pastiosity is genuine warmth and humor as well as a deep capacity for the enjoyment and appreciation of new situations.

Normal Pastiosity.

[handwriting sample]

Extreme Pastiosity. Many blobs of ink with occasional smearing and sometimes ink-filled ovals characterize this writing. These writers are physically oriented, sensual, attracted to pleasurable activities and intensely absorbed in their own experiences. Artists, musicians and others who work in areas meaningfully creative to themselves can express their sensuality through their work and interpersonal relationships. However, when there is no creative or emotional outlet, a person can become undisciplined in seeking sensual pleasure. Thus the pastiose writer who is deeply inhibited or externally thwarted will exhibit the negative characteristics of his inherent sensuality.

For example, pastiosity which produces ink-filled ovals shows a personality capable of explosive outbursts. The anxiety produced from the repressed sexuality also makes the person guarded about natural self-expression. Or, the same anxiety in another personality may lead to the verbal expression of sexual innuendos.

Excessively pastiose writers can be distracted from the responsibilities of daily life or escape from them through sexual day-dreaming, alcohol, narcotic stimulation or psychosomatic illnesses. And they are far more likely to commit crimes of violence than are non-pastiose writers. Excessive pastiosity is often displayed in the writing of the physically or mentally ill.

[handwriting sample]

[handwritten text] you will have security in my former works, as well as security prospective, in the one to come, (The Tortoise-Hunters) because if you accede to the aforesaid request; this letter shall be your voucher, that I am willing your house should publish it, on the old basis — half-profits.

Reply immediately, if you please,

And Believe Me, Yours

Herman Melville

SHARP WRITING

Those who manage a very clean writing stroke are restrained and reserved, spiritual and idealistic. At their highest, they are refined and sensitive, placing more importance upon mental processes than upon emotional feelings. They are usually verbally articulate and discriminating, projecting a sense of subtlety, nuance and irony. They are mentally intense but convey the impression of physical weakness, which may or may not be true. In any case, they save their physical strength for when it is needed.

On the minus side, sharp writers are cold, resentful and somewhat unable to enjoy their experiences. Inner remoteness, rigidity and a lack of ability to relate on a physical level contribute to their special brand of loneliness. Idealistically, they see themselves as heroes.

[handwritten text] many more years of tennis. Glad to be here to help celebrate,

Remember, when judging pressure, to consider all three aspects:

The intensity or depth—this force tells you how much energy is available for work or goal-directed pursuits.

The width of the stroke—the relative thinness or thickness of the stroke tells you how the writer displays energy in action.

The pastiosity of the stroke—the relative pastiosity or sharpness of the inking pattern tells you how sensual or spiritual the writer is.

Alla bella e graziosa

Marie Dupocke

l'amico

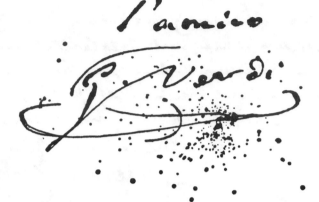

GIUSEPPE VERDI,
Italian composer.

... menage in New York he write him you the address because of our work. nearer to own success in America, a sooner edition of these articles.

Yours sincerely truely

Adler.

DR. ALFRED ADLER,
German born
psychologist.

MARQUIS DE SADE, French
soldier and pervert.

GIOVANNI CASANOVA,
Italian adventurer and lover.

Votre tres humble, et tres obéissant Serviteur Casanova

... Casanova

BETTINA VON ARNIM.

46

much obliged & humble servant.

Js Newton.

ISAAC NEWTON,
English natural
philosopher and
mathematician.

Emma Hamilton

LADY HAMILTON, Mistress of
Lord Nelson.

H. Himmler.

HEINRICH HIMMLER,
Nazi Gestapo chief.

*Dear Friend —
You will be
seeing more of me
soon in —
"Let's Make Love"*

MARILYN MONROE,
Actress and legend.

Marilyn

*I have only to say that
I have been more than
one hundred times
engaged in Battle*

Horatio Nelson

LORD HORATIO NELSON,
English military commander.
Written with his
right hand.

Written with his left
hand 10 years after
losing the right hand
in battle.

*May the God of Justice
crown my endeavours
with success*

Nelson & Bronte

47

Trist Longpay Place de la Concorde, Paris.

With love, and the very best wishes, to all,

Tom Wolfe

THOMAS WOLFE,
Writer.

BALZAC,
French novelist.

*notre admiration aujourd'hui
nous lui sommes attachés par
des liens plus étroit et plus
doux ceux de l'amitié et de
la reconnoissance.
ce 1er février 1792   Marie Antoinette*

MARIE ANTOINETTE, Queen of France.
Sample penned while in prison.

at least! If so, let me hear from you again. Sincerely,

Henry Miller

HENRY MILLER, American writer.

Size and Spacing

The person's use of letter size gives us an idea of how much importance he places upon himself and upon his own actions. It is an indication of how the writer will impress himself upon his environment. For example, the large writer approaches life with extroversion and extravagance and the small writer with reclusiveness and modesty. Letter size shows the writer's unconscious feelings about relating to other people.

HOW TO MEASURE SIZE

To determine the size of a handwriting sample look principally at the middle zone letters. These should be 1/8th of an inch or 3 millimeters high to fall within the normal, copy-book, category. Writing in which the middle zone letters rise consistently above 1/8th of an inch is considered larger than normal and anything smaller than 1/8th of an inch is held to be smaller than normal.

Normal or Average Copy-Book Size. People who write with a normal sized script can be expected to fit into conventional or prevailing circumstances with adaptability and balance of mind. They are practical and realistic.

1/8"

I never got Georgia's address — please send it to me..

Larger than Average Size handwriting shows the writer's need to make an impression, to be observed, to win recognition. These people need and enjoy attention and admiration; they do not like to be alone. They can act with boldness, enthusiasm, and optimism, but are also capable of boastfulness, restlessness, and lack of concentration and discipline.

Sorry I never see you; I've moved down to the beach a great new house — or great house I should say. It's on

Smaller than Average Size handwriting denotes an introspective person, one not apt to seek the limelight and who is not very communicative except with close friends. Small writers often have an academic mentality and can concentrate for long periods of time in their studies and projects. Although they are modest, sometimes to the point of feelings of inferiority, the talent of these writers for detail and for organizing often gives them good executive ability.

Surprisingly, a number of small script writers are not retiring persons, but rather, possess a strong power drive. They are quite independent of what others think.

Again, thank you very much for the glorious afternoon last Friday! I so enjoyed champagne at your house and lunch at the l'Ermitage — a true fête.

Variable Letter Sizes, that is, middle zone letters ranging in size from 1/16th of an inch upwards, show a writer who is emotionally off-balance a good deal of the time and thus inconsistent in his responses to other people and to his environment. Too much caught up in his own feelings, he is likely to be self-centered, overly-expressive, indecisive, and childish. Those around him often find him moody and immature, but not always without charm.

for is in good shape, I think! Separation cum friendship settles well with both of us. Love

Measuring Breadth or Width of letter size. Look at the small letter "n." It is normal for this letter to make a square; in narrow writing it will be compressed and in broad writing it will be extended.

SPACING WITHIN WORDS

When a person writes a single letter he represents himself. If he makes a narrow letter form he can be expected to be narrow-minded about himself, that is, judgmental, up-tight, or self-conscious. If he makes a broad letter form he can be expected to be inwardly broad-minded with himself, generously giving himself room to be natural and to grow.

The distance that the writer places between the letters shows how he relates on a personal level to other people. If he is cautious or introverted the letters will be crowded close to each other, craving contact. Movement is inward, back to the individual's own ego.

sugar is sweet and so are you

If the writer is outgoing, expansive, and is not inhibited with others, it will be reflected in wide letters spaced farther apart. This person is extroverted, and moves outward toward society.

sugar is sweet and so

The combination of narrow letters with wide spaces between them is sometimes termed a typically American handwriting characteristic and is often found in feminine handwriting. This is a person who appears to be very outgoing (wide connecting strokes) but is inwardly up-tight and cautious with his feelings (narrow letters).

sugar is sweet and so

The combination of wide letter forms with narrow spaces between them reveals a person who gives himself latitude but crowds others. This writer can be egocentric and self-centered much the same as the middle zone emphasis writer or the person who communicates in printed capitals.

sugar is sweet and so are you

A normal, well-balanced spacing within the letter shapes and between them shows a personality that is balanced and flexible in relationship to others, with the ability for both closeness and reserve where appropriate.

sugar is sweet and so are you

SPACING BETWEEN WORDS

The space left between the written words represents the distance that the writer would like to maintain between himself and society at large. Once again, as with the single letter, the writer is representing himself as he places each word unit on the page; between the words lies the distance he needs for emotional comfort with others, his territorial boundaries.

Very narrow spaces between the words show someone who will crowd others for attention, craving constant contact and closeness. Such a writer can be selfish in his demands and unwilling to give of his own time and energies to others.

sugar is sweet and so are you

Very wide spaces between words indicate the writer's need to maintain his distance from social contact, either due to an inner need for privacy or to a tendency toward isolation sometimes reinforced by difficulty in communicating with others.

sugar   is   sweet   and   so   are

The combination of narrow letters with cramped spacing between the words shows a person who is fearful and dependent, who cannot give himself (or others) enough space in life. Through inhibition or need this writer will impose blindly on others. Often these people cannot see the forest for the trees.

sugar is sweet and so are you

The combination of wide letters with wide spaces between the words denotes a person who demands attention in an extravagant or exaggerated manner, stemming from a need to be noticed, to be important.

sugar   is   sweet   and

Remember that well-balanced spacing always gives evidence of the writer's social maturity, intelligence, and inner organization. He will be able to deal flexibly and objectively with himself and with other people.

sugar is sweet and so are you

SPACING BETWEEN LINES

The amount of space that the writer leaves between the lines on the page gives clues to the orderliness and clarity of his thinking, and to the amount of interaction that he wishes to have with his environment. Normal spacing has its own personal harmony and flexibility.

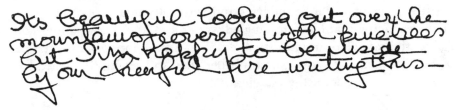

The more crowded and tangled a line is within itself or with those above and below, the more confused are the writer's thoughts and feelings. The inner pressure of many emotional reactions puts this type of individual in constant need of expressing himself in words, actions, projects. Such writers are lively, forceful, and often creative, but can suffer from a lack of clarity of purpose or from jumbled ideas and poor concentration.

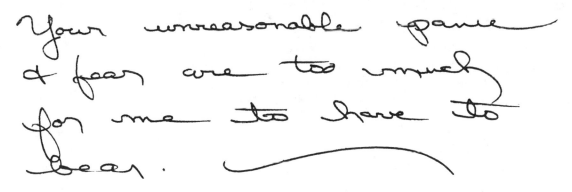

The writer who sets his lines far apart from each other on the page is isolating himself from his environment, socially, psychologically, or both. He has grown to fear contact and closeness. Or he may have constructed grandiose fantasies for himself that set him apart from others, or he may harbor suspicions and hostilities that keep him separate and untrusting. Distance between lines is also an indication of extravagance, just as crowding can mean stinginess.

RIGID AND IRREGULAR SPACING

Rigid, machine-like placement of letters, words, and lines on the page indicates conscious or unconscious overcontrol on the part of a writer who is in fear of losing control of himself or of his surroundings. He hides behind a carefully arranged facade of "beautiful" letter forms and planned spaces.

and may you and
your loved ones
enjoy all of God's
richest blessings
in 1976.

Affectionately,

Irregular spacing on the page is a clue to an inwardly unsettled character in conflict with its social self, friendly one minute and withdrawn the next. Such a person has little sense of social boundaries and is usually unaware of his own moodiness. Uneven spacing that leads to tangled words and lines shows inner confusion, lack of objectivity, lack of organization, emphasis upon fantasy, and self-centeredness. In the lower zone, it shows an unfulfilled love and sexual life which have been transposed into the realm of the imagination.

MARGINS

The page is space, and the way that the individual fills his page with script shows how he will approach the world. The left side of the paper represents the past from which the writer starts, and the right side symbolizes his goals and the future. Placement on the page also shows the quality of the person's taste, his social, cultural, and artistic tendencies, or a lack of these. And, unconscious feelings toward space and its use give clues to the person's self-esteem and how he will relate to others.

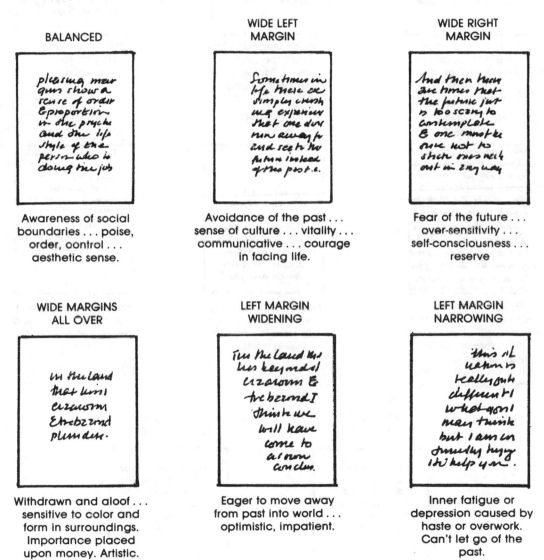

BALANCED

Awareness of social boundaries . . . poise, order, control . . . aesthetic sense.

WIDE LEFT MARGIN

Avoidance of the past . . . sense of culture . . . vitality . . . communicative . . . courage in facing life.

WIDE RIGHT MARGIN

Fear of the future . . . over-sensitivity . . . self-consciousness . . . reserve

WIDE MARGINS ALL OVER

Withdrawn and aloof . . . sensitive to color and form in surroundings. Importance placed upon money. Artistic.

LEFT MARGIN WIDENING

Eager to move away from past into world . . . optimistic, impatient.

LEFT MARGIN NARROWING

Inner fatigue or depression caused by haste or overwork. Can't let go of the past.

NARROW MARGINS BOTH SIDES

Stinginess or acquis-
itiveness . . . lack of
consideration and
reserve.

UNEVEN LEFT MARGIN

Defiance and rebellion
toward the rules of
society . . . lack of inner
order and balance.

UNEVEN RIGHT MARGIN

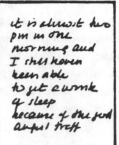

Impulsive moods . . .
acts and reactions
unreliable.

NO MARGINS ANYWHERE

Writer eliminates all
barriers between himself
and others . . . causes strong
negative or positive
reactions in others . . .
talks too much . . . fears
empty spaces or death.

WIDE UPPER MARGIN

Modesty and formality . . .
respect being shown
toward the person
being written to.

NARROW UPPER MARGIN

Informality, directness
of approach . . . lack of
respect, indifference.

WIDE LOWER MARGIN

Losing interest in one's
environment . . . idealism . . .
aloofness . . . reserve.

NARROW LOWER MARGIN

Desire to communicate . . .
materialism . . . sentimental,
sometimes depressed.

ENVELOPES

Envelopes, like pages, represent an area of space upon which the writer takes a personal position that reveals traits of his personality and his relationships with others. Addresses on envelopes are public ego manifestations for the writer, similar to signatures, with a good number of capital letters that can be embellished or personalized.

When the writing on the envelope is consistent in size and form with that of the letter inside, the writer will behave pretty much the same way in public as he does in private. Over-embellishment or false show on the envelope is ostentatious and deliberately misleading. Naturally, legibility and control in addressing envelopes is of first importance.

A. Level Head
Straight street
Judicious, Ohio

Norma Reason
21 Sensible street
Temperance, Va. 02664

LEGIBLE . . . ordered mind . . .
adaptible, cooperative.

Jes Careful
Hit or Miss
mississippi

Miss Taken
473 any street
LA 94026

ILLEGIBLE . . . confused mind . . .
inability to conform . . . anti-social.

Merry Goround
208 Freedom Way
Eagerness, New York
35021

TOO FAR RIGHTWARD . . .
escaping past . . . impulsive . . . restless.

Contessa Contrary
Rue de Morose
Barca Lonely, Italy

Miss Ima Fraid
Yesterday Valley,
Utah, U.S.A.

TOO FAR LEFTWARD . . .
clings to past . . . reserved.

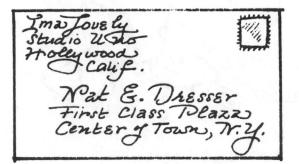

OVER-EMBELLISHED . . . phony
facade . . .desire for fame.

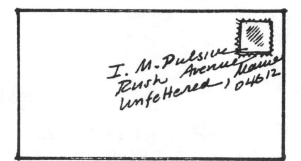

WORDS RUN INTO STAMP . . .
hasty, careless . . . desires complete freedom.

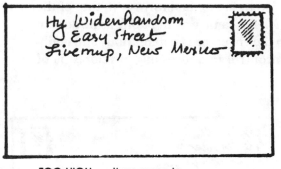

TOO HIGH . . . lives more in
fantasy than reality . . . detached . . .
lacks confidence.

TOO LOW . . . Pessimistic . . . cautious
depressed . . . suspecting.

Speed: The Pace of Writing

Writing speed increases naturally with practice, but no amount of practice can make a fluent writer out of a sluggish, overly self-conscious, or dim-witted person. The speed with which the person moves comfortably over the page reflects the tempo of his thinking, of his actions and his reactions. Is he "quick" or "slow"? His personal pace is a measure of his spontaneity and will affect his writing rhythm and form quality.

Curves are more easily written than straight lines, angles or broken lines, and tall letters flow more quickly from the pen than tiny ones. Dots are hard to make at high speed and tend to turn into commas and dashes. The urge toward spontaneity slants the writing to the right, whereas hesitancy draws the hand back toward an upright or leftward slant. Pressure that alternates naturally is more quickly and smoothly performed than extremely light or heavy lines.

Be on the watch for a change of writing pace in individual words where the writer has instinctively hesitated; also look for an increase in pace as the writer's emotions are aroused. Key words and phrases have a way of changing pace and position subtly on the page. The faster the writing the more the size tends to increase and the strokes to reach out and forward, but no matter how fast, the writing should not lose its legibility, its power to communicate.

loops on y type letters means hostility I've noticed that.. I'm not making as many letters with /out Loops —!

Slower than Average Writing generally appears conventional, over-elaborate, or clumsy. The stroke is overly controlled or hesitant, or can be tremulous, jerky, and retouched. The connective forms are more often arcades and angles, and the slant is upright to leftward. Letters are very small or very large, their shapes narrow or sprawled out. Ends of words may increase in size, loops are enlarged, and there is much made of details and flourishes. The pressure is either barely sufficient or excessive, the strokes unmodulated in width. The rhythm and form level are poor overall.

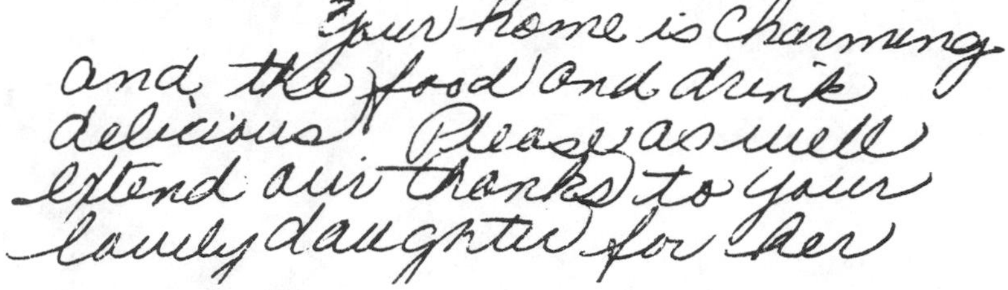

[handwritten sample]

Faster than Average or Speedy Writing will have an unadorned, spontaneous and natural look. The pattern will be animated and rhythmic with smooth, unbroken strokes and outward swinging curves. The directional trend will be rightward with the i dots streaklike and placed to the right of the stem or linked to the next letter, and the t bars extended, placed to the right of the stem. Connective forms are garland or threadlike and the letters streamlined and of medium size. Endings of words can become threadlike and there is an overall neglect of detail and flourish.

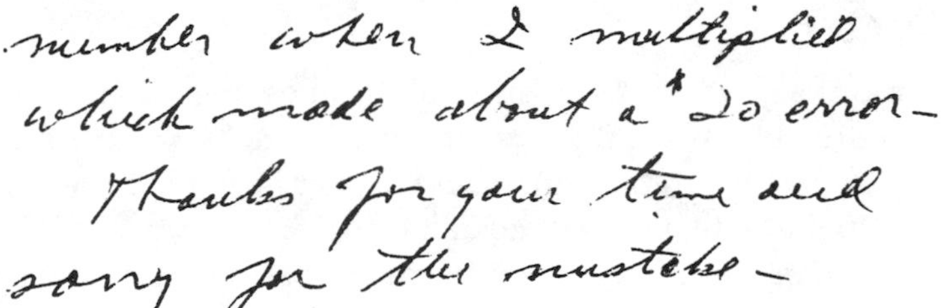

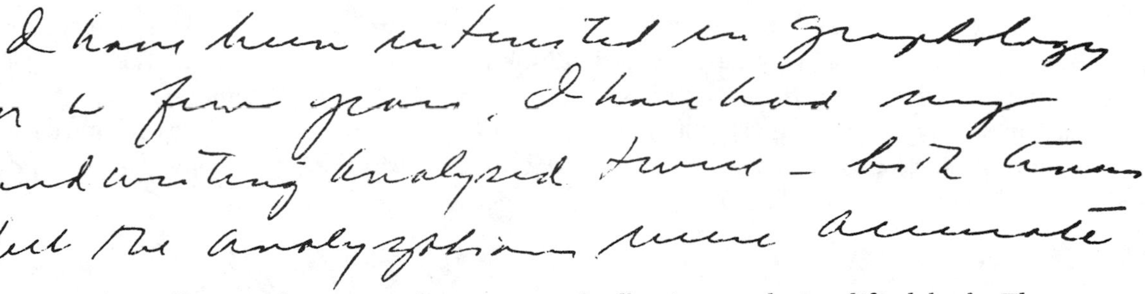

[handwritten sample]

[handwritten sample]

A naturally speedy writing has a smooth, flowing, and simplified look. The graphologist finds speed vital to understanding the writer's personality; it shows the level of spontaneity in personal response and the practicality of character. A quick legible hand is partly a matter of experience and manual skill, but it always shows mature and intelligent simplification of letter forms. The natural, open individual will write with a time-saving simplicity and with grace. Speed gives impetus to the individualization of letter forms as the writer unconsciously creates his own smooth shortcuts. Such forms can be highly original.

Slow writing is almost always suspect of calculation, self-consciousness, even stupidity and dishonesty. Elaboration and exaggeration give so many negative clues to personality; neither is possible in a speedy hand. Nor is there time for touching up, coiling, tangling, breaks, reversed pressure and extraneous leftward motions, all signs of mental disorder. In its role of producing a simple and sophisticated hand, speed is a necessary part of good rhythm and form quality.

Bon pour un cadeau de jour de l'an, que je paierai, dès ma rentrée à Paris, sur la présentation de ce billet.

Décembre 98 Emile Zola

EMILE ZOLA, Author.

explain what passed between them. We might have seen David Joriszs, who used to be the true Christ, in Delft. Three years after he died, his corpse was take out at the stake. Jacob Theelstinski proclaimed himself in Poland. Ezekiel ? ah Sträßel, Hans Keyl of Gerlingen, and Philippus Ziegler, Christina R erin, were others who made prophecy, or proclaimed themselves

SACHEVERELL SITWELL, Author.

Thank you for asking a sample of my handwriting.

Joan Crawford

JOAN CRAWFORD, Actress.

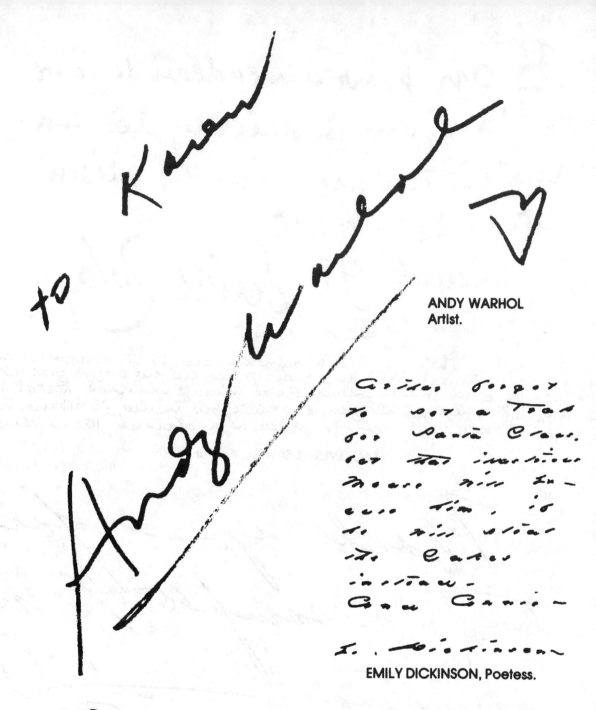

ANDY WARHOL
Artist.

EMILY DICKINSON, Poetess.

That shook when he laughed, like a bowlfull of jelly.
He was chubby and plump, a right jolly old elf,
And I laughed when I saw him, in spite of myself;
A wink of his eye and a twist of his head,

CLEMENT MOORE, Poet.

Clement C. Moore.

62

a good job it will

because the plains are

Amelia Earhart

AMELIA EARHART
Aviatrix.

Jimmy Carter

Rosalynn Carter

JIMMY CARTER
ROSALYN CARTER,
President and wife.

quelques jours et je
vous écrirai.

a vous de coeur

GEORGE SAND
Author.

G Sand

22.8.63.

our new school year has opened up
and we are hoping for good results.
In addition to getting the funds for
our usual expenses an effort is to going to
give my self to increase our
endowment fund.

yours truly

BOOKER WASHINGTON,
Educator.

Booker T. Washington,

63

Rhythm and Form Quality

Each handwriting has its own unique rhythm. Like heartbeats and light waves, handwriting shows a regular recurrence and alteration of features. The writer's success at achieving unity and harmony within the self and in relation to the world at large is revealed in the over-all balance and form quality of his writing.

To determine the rhythm of a sample hold the page up in front of you and allow yourself to react to the total impression that the pattern of written strokes produces. Remember that the two major principles of rhythm are *repetition* and *change*. Beware of a rigid machine-like quality which suggests an anxious, up-tight character who fears loss of balance. On the other extreme recognize in an uneven, fragmented, or neglected script an unstable personality expressing itself.

Since rhythm is a subtle over-view comprised of many individual factors, rating its quality requires practice and sensitivity. As an aid, keep in mind the following handwriting characteristics:

Height.   The letter zones. Look for balance between the upper, the middle and the lower zones.

Width.   Examine the breadth of the letters, the distances between letters, words, lines, the length of the connecting strokes, and the slant of the writing.

Spacing.   How does the writing fit on the page? Notice the margins and the space between lines and the balance between the height and the width of the letters.

Depth.   Feel the pressure on the paper and try to determine the direction of the stroke from the width of the upstrokes and the downstrokes.

The combination of these spatial characteristics on the page: margins; spaces between lines, words and letters; plus the forms of the letters themselves determine the rhythmic symmetry of the sample. These writing characteristics demonstrate the balance, variety and richness of the personality.

In keeping with the basic principle of rhythm, repetition and change, good form quality of the letters requires that they not be too rounded, nor too angular, threaded, arcaded, or even too closely tied to the schoolbook Palmer method. On the other hand, many so-called "beautiful" writings are the ornamented or artificial products of those wishing to appear artistic or unusual in some way.

Naturally, it takes time looking at many handwritings to begin to judge successfully the quality of the rhythm and the form level. Sometimes this is an aesthetic judgment that will be influenced by the personal values of the analyst. Some react favorably to more conventional forms, others look for original letter shapes. Above all, most graphologists value writing that is not artificial or rigid and are suspicious of extreme mixtures of graphological elements. Regulated handwriting can be rhythmical providing it is not rigidly artificial. True genius personalities, such as Leo Tolstoy and Beethoven, tend to create their own exceptional form level and rhythm.

LUDWIG VON BEETHOVEN

LEO TOLSTOY

The Form Quality of the letters is such an important part of the rhythm of the writing that it deserves special mention. Letter form quality is determined by the contour, shape, ornamentation, curvature, progression of stroke (ie: backwards or forwards), and speed of execution. Naturally, legibility is a primary consideration, even with speedy writers.

The spine of the letter (the downstroke) is drawn by contracting the hand muscles. Therefore, it is likely to be more static and an indication of inner character and strength. In contrast, the upstroke is created by a release of muscles, is lighter in pressure, and gives a fluid variety to the letter forms.

This primary overall evaluation of rhythm and form quality gives the graphologist a yardstick in deciding whether to interpret a specific sign in the writing in a positive or a negative way. For example: is a very light-pressured hand indicative of neurotic impressionability and lack of energy, or of spirituality and responsive sensitivity? The evaluation of the aesthetics of the rhythm and form quality will provide the base for a positive or a negative interpretation. Even the most intuitive graphologist should beware of interpreting specific letter characteristics out of the context of the entire writing, just as one should not evaluate a signature separately from a portion of the text.

Again, enjoy your Christmas + we'll see you on New Years Eve.

Healthy Mature Rhythm and Form Quality. Notice the well-balanced height width, pressure, and spacing. This poised, relaxed, and smoothly written character reflects the writer's inner harmony.

Unrhythmic Writing with Poor Letter Form Quality. In the three samples below observe the unstable slant and spacing, the combination of stunted and exaggerated letter sizes, erratic baselines, uneven pressure and the disintegrated or overly-slow and elaborated letter forms. All samples show signs of neurotic immaturity, inner personality disorganization, and a lack of self-awareness and discipline.

I was born on March 3, 1951. It is up to you to tell me what I do, what my interests are and what my strong points are

Will I have money soon?

About four summers ago, my parents and I went on a sailing trip from St. Petersburg to the Florida keys. During our journey we encountered many problems with the weather. Everynight we would have a

Ornamentation and Neglect. As the writing style matures and develops away from the standard forms it can take two opposite directions, toward simplification or toward elaboration. A writer who values speed and economy of motion may streamline the letter form to its essential skeleton, a time-saving simplicity. If richness is valued, the writer will unconsciously add extra strokes to the letters, for garnish. Creative qualities are judged by how successfully the writer improves yet *simplifies* the script. As long as the writing is natural and spontaneous, smooth, unforced and unselfconscious, it will exhibit a good rhythm and form level.

The following sample displays a fine balance of good rhythm and form level. It is neither ornamental nor neglected and manages to convey a feeling of personal style within a traditional structure.

Graphology is the study of handwriting.

Overly Embellished Writing.   Showy and pretentious script is, like all extremes in handwriting, a facade or compensation for inner weakness. Ornamented strokes are slow to make, very self-conscious and reveal a contrived personality. The much-admired intellectual Greek "e" is slower to write than the Palmer type "e" and does not have a natural place in many scripts. Ornamented capital letters usually go beyond a respect for tradition, revealing the vain showman.

*of   last minute changes —
for instance ... Three of the orders started
within three days of booking them —*

Neglected Writing.   Simplification can reach an unrhythmic extreme for quite different reasons than speed or maturity. Remember that a simple and speedy script is a sign of maturity and purposefulness. Untended, careless, and half-completed letters and a neglected over-all look, however, arises from a disorganized and unfocused personality with depressive moods. Pressure, downhill baselines, and x-ing shows suicidal tendencies in the careless writer.

Neglected Writing

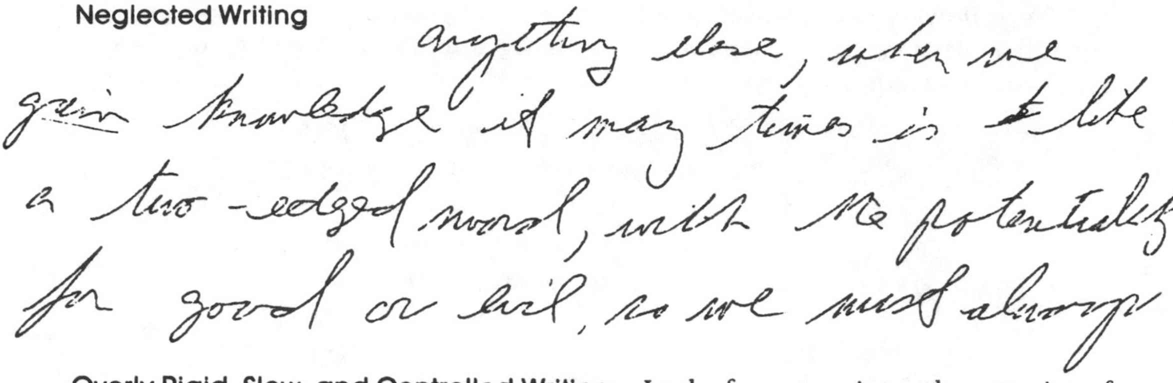
anything else, when we
gain knowledge it many times is like
a two-edged sword, with the potentiality
for good or evil, so we must always

Overly Rigid, Slow, and Controlled Writing. Lack of spontaneity and repression of communication interferes with good rhythm. This writer believes that he has something to hide or fears what he might do if he lost control, so he constructs a careful, self-protective script, usually a conventional or "beautiful" form. This is rigidly adhered to, and hides inner frustration and immaturity behind its machine-like regularity.

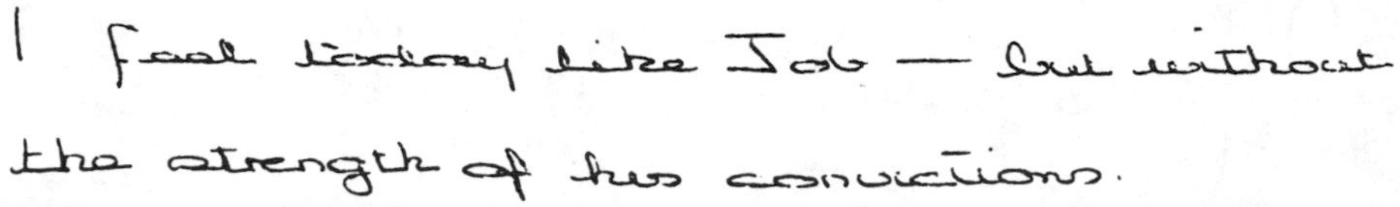
I feel lonely like Job — but without
the strength of his convictions.

Rhythmic Disturbance through Nervous Anxiety. Heedless, ill-formed letters, usually of a variety of sizes, written with erratic pressure, indicate anxiety. Tension in the hand will cause strokes to lighten suddenly, creating holes. Jerks and tics appear, parts of letters are missing. Often the anxious writer will mix cursive and printed script, make numerous mistakes, and tangle.

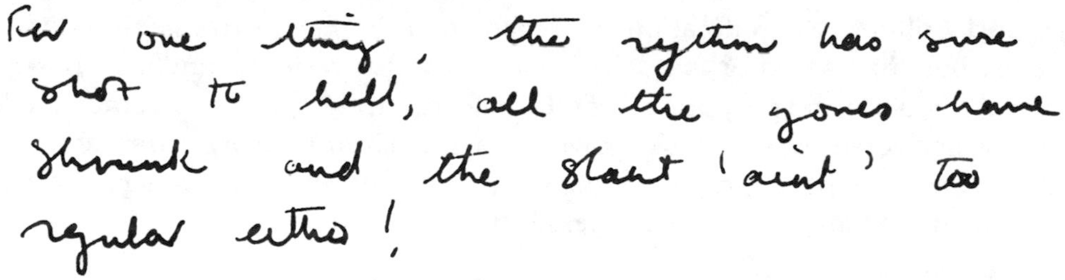
For one thing, the rythm has sure
shot to hell, all the zones have
shrunk and the slant 'aint' too
regular either!

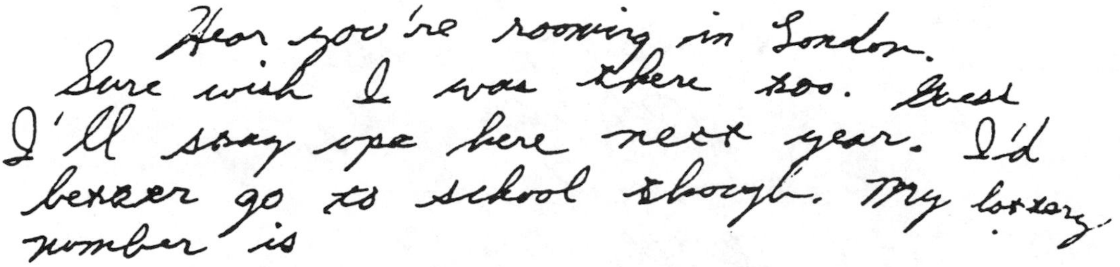
Hear you're rooming in London.
Sure wish I was there too. Guess
I'll stay here next year. I'd
better go to school though. My lottery
number is

Rhythmic Disturbance due to Old Age. Specific numerical age cannot be determined from handwriting, only emotional maturity can. It is natural, however, that the weakening muscles and eyesight of age will lead to slower, less-coordinated writing with shakiness and uneven or lighter pressure. Many older people suffer from depression, which shows in drooping baselines; others toward the end of their lives intensify religious feelings and will emphasize upward strokes at the end of words, looking heavenward for answers. Preoccupation with the body leads to swelling lower loops.

It is difficult to separate the signs of normal aging from those of physical illness. The aged writer who feels well shows few rhythm changes, and the aged writer who is ill will have illness features overshadowing the natural decline of age.

What Tongue can speak its comprehensive Grace?

What Thought its Depths unfathomable trace?

Above is the nineteenth century Spencerian script of a twenty year-old man. Below is the same writer at the age of sixty-eight.

The gift of Uncle Topham to his nephew W E Soper July 2 — 1888

Below is the writing of a vigorous seventy year-old man.

I am most happy to be here tonight - as this my sons 40th birthday

RHYTHM AND FORM LEVEL: PHYSICAL ILLNESS, DRUGS, AND ALCOHOL

Physical Illness. Injury to the body most often changes the rhythm and form quality in the zone of the writing which corresponds to the injured area. Heart disease, circulatory problems, and nerve disease distribute their signs throughout the zones. Sometimes the t bars of sick people become longer and stronger as their will to live is kindled; details like periods are omitted by some writers through fatigue, anxiety, or a growing fear of endings. Anxious preoccupation with body functions leads to swelling of lower zone loops, erratic pressure, shakes and tremors, and signs of depression.

The best way to distinguish physical illness from writing disturbance of mental origin is to have samples to compare from different periods in the writer's life; most of all, physical problems will affect the pressure pattern and the smoothness of the letter strokes.

MIDDLE BODY INJURY. Broken and repaired middle zone letters . . . erratic middle zone letter size and shape . . . MZ threading and falling, depressed words.

By now you should be back from your trip to India. Do let me know how it went and if you enjoyed it.

NERVE DAMAGE. Erratic pressure . . . tremulous and jerky strokes . . . poor spacing . . . slow, overly-controlled letter forms.

I don't know exactly what to write but perhaps you can read something in this.

HEART DISEASE AND CIRCULATORY PROBLEMS. Dotting and blobs with slow, uneven pressure . . . lower loops bent and enlarged . . . pastiosity, light spots, bends, jerks, tics, tangling and depression.

windshield — but the plane cracked in half and Bill went down into the frigid water — and they couldn't get a breath out with all the

HEALTHY WRITING. Good pressure pattern . . . relaxed strokes . . . clear spacing and balanced zone.

& we had such a good time .. thanks again. I am embarassed to find

Drug detection in handwriting is complicated by its similarity to nervous problems. Minor tranquilizer users have difficulty writing on a level line and keeping even spacing and letter size; mistakes occur, particularly in halts or breaks in the connecting strokes along the baseline.

The stronger anti-depressants and mood-changing drugs cause tiny uncontrollable jerks of the hand. These produce sudden and obvious mistakes and weirdly-shaped letters. The pressure is very uneven, slant varies at random, and angular shapes thrust suddenly next to rounded ones. Letters rise and fall unexpectedly. Overall the rhythm pattern shows evenness punctuated by abrupt and noticeably bizarre tremors and mistakes.

MINOR TRANQUILIZERS. Uncontrollable jerks of the hand cause mistakes and sudden odd shapes . . . angularity appears abruptly next to roundness . . . letters change size or rise and fall unexpectedly . . . pressure is uneven with tremors.

I would enjoy greatly working on a more lot. perhaps getting a glimpse from time to time of how things are really done

MAJOR TRANQUILIZERS. Hospitalized patient on the drug, Thorazine . . . extreme disintegration.

Past now is the 9th over the fever left her they Graham believe that I had heald your daughter. spirit is stronger.

Alcohol. Most alcoholics, no matter how talented or successful, are inadequate personalities; they usually have a poor self-image and a critical, easily-frustrated nature, capable of emotional extremes. Reality is often painful for these people; the numbing fantasy world of alcohol offers escape from anxiety and tension.

In the writing look for signs of immaturity: lead-in strokes, weak and varied t-bars, over-inflated, emotional loops. The inner critic at work against himself and others is disclosed in points at the baseline, tics, hooks and sword-like strokes. A functioning alcoholic will have fast and muddy but legible writing; impulsive and relaxed, he still strives for control and communication.

and cheerful. Night after night of sitting here in the coma inn drinking is leaving me as bent as a five-penny nail

The immediate effect of alcohol on rhythm and form quality is likely to be more disintegrating to the non-alcoholic who has little tolerance for the drug than to the habitual drinker who has learned to hide his problem. In general, expect to find: increase in pressure, tremors, breaks between the letters, sloppiness and mistakes, with pastiosity; inability to keep the spacing between the letters even; erratic pressure pattern; wider loops and longer connecting strokes; a sad, threaded middle zone or a depressed baseline; an overall jerkiness and disintegration in both rhythm and form quality.

friendly hostess - person - and at the moment I am salivating at the thought of that 'outta sight' rice and salad - not to

be mine — If there is anything wanting which is with-
in my power to give, do not fail to let me know it.
And now with a brave Army, and a just cause, may
God sustain you.

**ABRAHAM
LINCOLN**

Yours very truly
A. Lincoln

MICHELANGELO, Artist.

Sia noto chome io michelagniolo buonarvoti o ueduto
oggi questo di uentitre di nouebro 1529 un chauallo
baio cho sun fornimeti a micholo di mactes chauall
e della S di firezo p scudi octo dequali menne

To
"Cookie –
eater"
from

"Cookie –
Maker"...
See you soon!

25 YR. OLD WOMAN

Sigm. Freud

**SIGMUND FREUD
(Signature enlarged).**

73

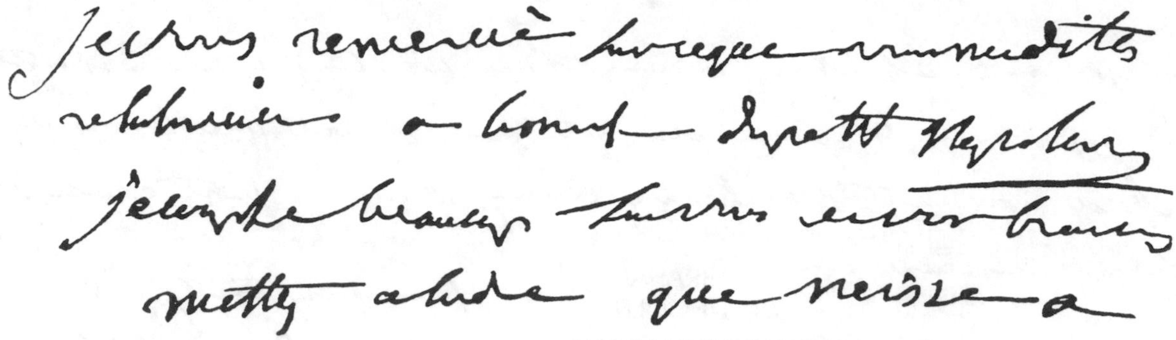

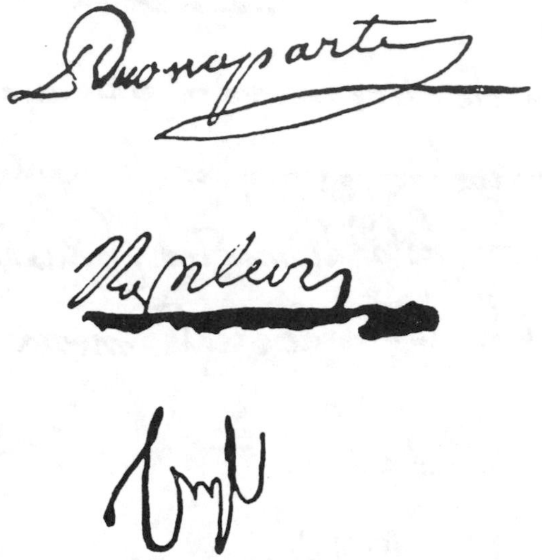

NAPOLEON BONAPARTE, with three deteriorating signatures.

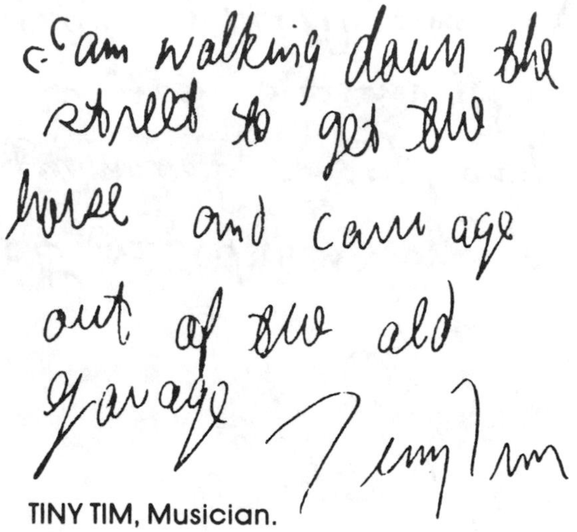
I am walking down the street to get the horse and carriage out of the old garage Tiny Tim

TINY TIM, Musician.

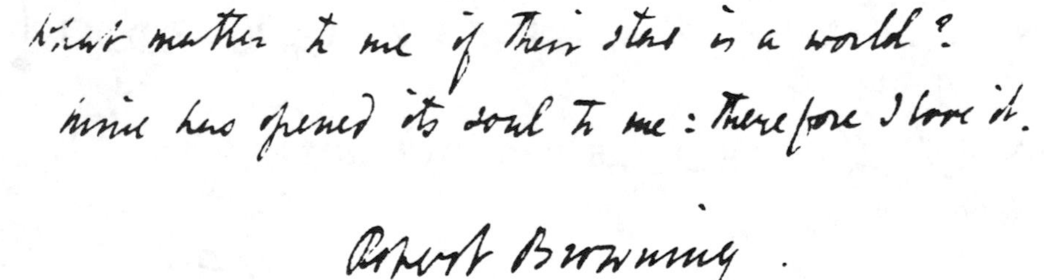
What matter to me if their star is a world?
Mine has opened its soul to me: therefore I love it.

Robert Browning.

ROBERT BROWNING, Poet.

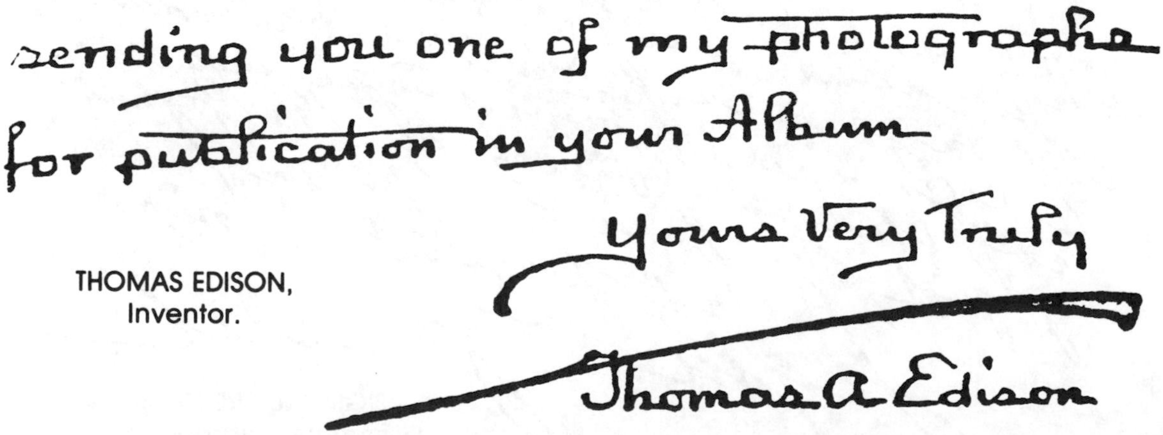
sending you one of my photographs
for publication in your Album
Yours Very Truly
Thomas A Edison

THOMAS EDISON, Inventor.

1958

Elvis A. Presley

1977

ELVIS PRESLEY,
Deterioration
in signature.

I am wolfingtown the short
I get the horse and carriage
out of the old garage

Floyd B. Odum

FLOYD ODUM,
Parkinson's
Disease.

Let each new temple, nobler than the last,
Shut thee from heaven with a dome more vast,
Till thou at length art free,
Leaving thine outgrown shell by life's unresting sea!

Oliver Wendell Holmes

OLIVER WENDELL HOLMES,
Poet, late in life.

at all the Tungsten we
have. WE can repair our
old mills & go ahead with
them. Until we build a
big new mills
Better address me. of Denver
Post Denver Rock W F Cody

BUFFALO BILL CODY,
Entertainer,
late in life.

Strokes & Shapes

There are two basic graphic movements which trace two distinct kinds of shapes. One is *curved* movement. The other is *straight* movement.

CURVED MOVEMENT

The circle is the perfect curved shape. In handwriting, oval letters and loops are formations of the circle. Many letters are comprised of parts of a circle.

The circle is a symbol of the eternal, perfect and cyclic nature of the universe. It represents the forces of nature and all aspects of the physical body, emotion and feeling. It is a loving container of intuitive, instinctive creativity and is the unification of the female force and the male force as expressed by the yin/yang principle. Things made up of circles are atoms, molecules, cells, plant and animal shapes, the earth and other planets, the sun, solar system, stars, galaxies—in short, the physical universe in its entirety.

The Circle and its Components. Arrows indicate the usual directional trends as seen in middle and upper zone letters. Lower zone letters are seen as reflections of what is above the baseline and are therefore reversed in their directional trend.

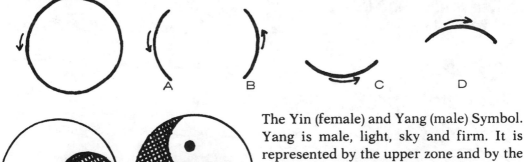

The Yin (female) and Yang (male) Symbol. Yang is male, light, sky and firm. It is represented by the upper zone and by the Right. Yin is female, dark, earth and yielding. It is represented by the lower zone and by the Left. In the illustrations above, B and D are male formations while A and C are female formations.

76

THE GARLAND FORMATION

A line of garlands looks like this.

Letter "r"—

Letter "t"—

Letter "m"—

The quickest and most natural way to form or correct a letter is with a garland, the movement being both rhythmic and practical. The garland stroke is the lower arc of a circle. It is concave in shape, like a cup or an open hand, and indicates an open, receptive and responsive nature.

Generally Garlanded Writing

Garland writers are passive and non-competitive. In their desire to avoid conflict, they can compromise themselves by taking the easy way out. These people like the visible, real world, and though friendly and kindhearted, don't quite understand the subtle undertones of situations. Socially, they are adaptable and flexible, but their strong need for security makes them feel threatened by any changes in their home, family or lifestyle. These types are expressive yet conventional. They want communication with and acceptance by other people.

Shallow Garlands. Of all writing formations, shallow garlands are the fastest and easiest to make. In their avoidance of the lower zone, people who make these strokes reveal character tendencies of shallowness, thoughtlessness, lack of concern and even indifference. They prefer the tangible world, and shun the mystical, the deep, or the unconscious. In their impulsive recklessness to reach goals, they can roll right over a less hasty person. They make much of connecting to others, but without deep feeling.

Clothesline Garlands. In their eagerness to express themselves and to communicate with others, these writers can come on too strong. At times, their behavior can be termed exhibitionistic. This is sometimes to distract others from noticing the difficulty they have in facing up to emotional situations.

Clothesline Garlands.

the Other + young son as secretary

Deep Garlands.   These writers give up some of their horizontal mobility, and in doing so, place more emphasis on contemplation and the inner world. They are impressionable, sentimental, sedate, sympathetic and conservative. They have a hard time giving up possessions, and are often collectors.

It is a beautiful evening. The food is excellent and one can notice all the attention to detail that went

Droopy Garlands.   Here the garland has been carried to extremes. These writers are too passive for their own good. Guilt feelings make it difficult for them to express their anger, and they wind up being someone's doormat or dish-rag. This is one indication of the masochistic personality.

has the Mumps. I sent her a get well card+ im also making her

This has been a

day full of fun and

Firm Garlands.   These writers express the qualities indicated by the garland formation. They handle life with ease, are demonstrative of their emotional nature, and respond in a warm and helpful fashion.

same letters differently. I always write

Weak Garlands. People who make weak, broken garland strokes lack follow-through. They have good intentions but their energy level is low. They are easily taken advantage of, are naive and gullible.

activities and volunteer work. How is everything

Sham Garlands. The garland with retracing can produce the sham formation. It indicates a socially repressed personality. The individual cannot express his aggressive feelings in a social situation, and will behave with charm and sweetness even when he doesn't like someone or something. It goes against his grain to be offensive, and even a bitter enemy can get a warm greeting in public. It's an indication often of a sly and cunning nature—one who can win without being tempermental.

he seemed mean to me. Mom

THE ARCADE FORMATION

A line of arcades looks like this.

Letter "r"—

Letter "t"—

Letter "m"—

The arcade stroke forms the upper part of a circle. Its shape is convex, like an arch or a roof, and provides support and structure. Generally speaking, arcaded writers are secretive, guarded, protective, resistant and proud.

As in the yin-yang principle, the arcade (yang) is the masculine counterpart to the feminine garland (yin). Arcaded writers are as protective and paternal as garland writers are receptive and maternal.

Generally Arcaded Writing

If life is a barbecue, let it be rare

Socially, the arcaded writer is a traditionalist, and wants to preserve what has already been established. He can get along with most personalities and finds the garland type quite pleasant. He has an artistic sense of proportion and is highly creative. Sometimes, he can be authoritarian, and offends with his seeming indifference to emotion. He's really just as emotional as the garland writer, but is very controlled in his expression of it. The arcaded writer can accept change, but it must be gradual. This type is not domineering, but neither is he to be dominated.

Personally, this writer is almost always eccentric. If everyone else is going one way (garlands are the most common stroke formation), he'll go the other. So it's really only in his desire to preserve social protocol that the arcaded writer is a traditionalist. Privately, he's a rebel. This type has a good memory, but does not absorb information quickly. He's serious, and generally needs a lot of time to make up his mind. Once it's made up, he'll stick with the decision.

Predominately Arcaded.   These people rely on instinct and intuition rather than on reason. They are watchful and defensive and can lack flexibility. They make good directors or heads of organizations and are fond of public speaking. When very arched, artistic qualities are present. On the negative side, this type can be too fascinated by intrigue, or can be involved in covering up or hushing over the true facts.

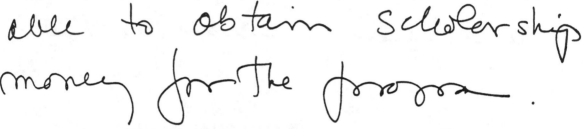

Wild or Big Arcades.   These wild flourishes are made by dramatic and theatrical people who wish to call attention to themselves. They have imagination, creative ability, and extreme pride. Often these extremes are covering feelings of inferiority with showiness.

Flat Arcades.   This formation acts more as a cover-up than as a protector. It has a sinuous and snaky quality to it and is an indication of an aloof, narrow-minded, rigid and hypocritical nature. This is a sign of dishonesty.

Retraced Arcades.   This person is feeling threatened. Behavior will be cautious, guarded, secretive, evasive and uptight.

CIRCULAR STROKES AND SHAPES

Exaggerated Roundness.   While it is considered normal for teenagers to write in a round style, adults who do so exhibit traits of childishness, immaturity, naivete and dependency in their personalities. Since roundness is a feminine trait, males who write a round style will display some feminine characteristics in their behavior. Round writers are flexible and yielding, preferring compromise to argument, yet regarding their home and family, they are possessive and jealous and will fight for these when their security is threatened. These types are emotional and physical, and find more fulfillment in the real world of experience than they could in the abstract realm of the mind.

Cows may come and cows may go, but the bull in this place goes on forever.

. This should be all "to be returned" are you going?

THE LOOP

This stroke is a combination of the arcade and the garland. It is thought of as a vessel in which emotion and feeling are contained.

Generally Loopy Writers.   These people place more emphasis on the emotional and feeling content of an experience than they do on the conceptual aspects of it. They are sympathetic, compassionate, and often quite intuitive in their understanding and response to situations in their environment. Their responses are impulsive more often than they are premeditated, and they will express in a verbal, sociable and extroverted manner. When creative, the loopy writer will produce realistic styles of art or will work with tangible goods.

I just remembered I was going to send you a sample of my handwriting

Normal Loops.   The emotional feelings being stored by the writer aren't excessive or scanty. This is an indication of emotional well-being.

I can express my feelings normally.

Exaggerated Loops.   When loops become extreme in their fullness, or appear everywhere, the person needs more and bigger vessels to store the excessive emotion being harbored. Feeling gets bottled up, because there isn't enough outlet for it. A key phrase here is *excessive emotional need.*

My emotions are all going crazy

Scanty Loops.   When writing contains short or meager loops, the writer has pared down his emotional feelings and needs smaller containers to store them. The ability to express emotion has been stunted.

I was put down a long time ago but I have

Retraced Loops. Some loops become so meager the upstrokes and downstrokes coincide, one lying on top of the other. Retracing reveals the person who is strongly inhibited emotionally to the extent that free expression of feeling is impossible. This writer is emotionally guarded.

Ever since I was hurt so badly, nobody

Distorted Loops.   When a loop deviates from its usual ovoid or circular shape to trace a twisted path, it reveals the emotionally distorted individual. Here it is important to consider the direction and shape of the distortion before determining the type and extent of the emotional problem.

My brothers did cruel things to

Reversed Loops.   Here emphasis is placed on doing the opposite of what is expected. The emotional nature is rebellious. This is one indication of amorality, dishonesty or other unconventional behavior.

Did you ever want your green scarf

Broken Loops.   Most of the time, broken loops will occur on the upstroke. (It is rare to see this on the downstroke. If you do, it is usually the result of a physical or mental illness.) When seen in the upstroke, a break is an indication of anxiety over a future course of action. The person doesn't feel sure of himself, and is uncertain of his ideas, relationships, or feelings.

Not feeling sure of my needs, I don't

Breaks at the tops of upper zone loops can indicate problems in the upper body or in the thinking processes. (Sample below.)

all the kings horses & all the kings men, couldn't put me together again,

Breaks at the bottoms of lower zone loops can indicate a lower body problem. Sometimes, women who have had a hysterectomy, or women who are menstruating will form these breaks.

Feeling rather empty in my body—

Tangled Loops. If the course of one loop interferes with the course of another, tangling results. This is an indication of emotional turbulence. The needs are confused, and the writer has a hard time sorting out feelings.

Honestly, I have felt so confused lately, it's

Leftward-Pulling Loops. These writers do not easily get over emotional wounds. They cling to old ways of being and are dependent on sustained relationships for emotional fulfillment. The leftward-pull indicates a preoccupation with the mother-figure and a lack of emotional maturity.

My mother? Well I guess it's hard to

Rightward-Pulling Loops. Attraction to the right reveals the ambitious go-getter. Here the emotional energy is directed to the pursuit of goals.

I guess youth is wasted on the young

Tall Loops. In the upper zone, tall loops indicate one who reaches for spiritual and conceptual emotional fulfillment. Emotions focus on the intangible, and fantasy and imagination are highlighted.

I'm the happiest when my head is

Long Loops. In the lower zone, extreme length denotes the individual who is physically restless and ready to explore new relationships and experiences. These writers need someone and something to touch.

life is more gratifying with bodily

THE OVAL

Ovals are found in the middle zone. They have to do with expression of emotion on a verbal and social level.

Normal Ovals contain one small loop on the right side and are lightly closed. These writers are honest yet discreet.

you can trust the normal oval

Open Ovals indicate a tendency to reveal too much. These people lack verbal caution. They are open and gullible.

Open ovals can say too much

Closed Ovals are naturally discreet without being secretive. They use tact and diplomacy in verbal expression.

Closed ovals are tactful and discreet

Tied Ovals have loops on both sides which overlap. This person is very cautious and guarded with verbal revelations.

Tied ovals are cautious and guard

Knotted Ovals are more extreme in formation and more verbally guarded than tied ovals. The more knotted the oval, the more secretive the writer. These people are inhibited and defensive verbally. This can lead to lying.

Knotted ovals are hiding some

Stabs in Ovals are a sign of a biting, sarcastic tongue. These writers manage to hurt people with their sharp words.

Stabs in ovals mean a sarcastic tongue

Explosive Ovals are made by those who have repressed their feelings to such a degree that they will suddenly explode in hostile, angry verbal tirades. These ovals are narrow and filled with ink.

People who repress their feelings can explode

Upside-Down Ovals are a reversal of the usual direction. As such, they indicate indirectness of approach and manipulative tendencies. Sometimes the intention isn't to deceive, but the insincerity results in misunderstanding.

Lack of direction can lead to deception

Ovals Broken at the Bottom are a sure sign of dishonesty, usually embezzling. These writers are cunning and deceitful.

broken at the bottom, dishonesty

Oval Letters Made in Two Parts are another indication of dishonesty. Be careful here though, because some European writing styles employ the two-part oval as a standard formation.

the person who makes ovals in two

This formation is a European method

STRAIGHT MOVEMENT

Straight movement results in vertical, horizontal or diagonal strokes, or in the shapes of the square, the cross, the triangle, or the X.

The straight line and the angular shape both symbolize human aspiration and the abstract mind. These strokes and shapes are sharp, aggressive, and energetic, having to do with the mental world. (The circle relates to the physical world.)

Straight movements are unbending and rigid. They convey authority, ambition and power. Man-made objects and structures are composed almost entirely of lines and angles.

Upstrokes and Rightward Strokes are released, expressive movement. The upstroke places emphasis on personal ambitions and aspirations (upper zone/intangible) while the rightward stroke places emphasis on action to and reaction from the environment (goal-directed pursuits). These strokes are associated with Yang, the male principal.

Downstrokes and Leftward Strokes are contracting and controlled movements. Here emphasis is placed on the self and on the development of inner abilities (vertical dimension aiming to the sphere of the lower zone) and also on the past and what is known and already experienced (the left). The Yin, or female principal is associated with these strokes.

THE ANGULAR FORMATION

A line of angles looks like this:

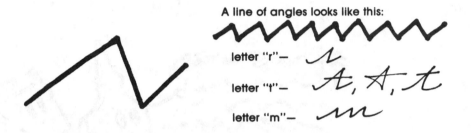

letter "r"—

letter "t"—

letter "m"—

This angle is comprised of two movements or gestures. For this reason, it is slower to write with angles than with garlands or arcades. It is an abrupt stroke, curt and precise, and as a garland might look like a waltz, the angle looks like a march.

Generally Angular Writing

I tell many tall tales, especially after a few (high balls).

I FEEL WE DON'T THINK ON THE SAME PLANE MUCH

We have already identified angularity with mental energy and with aggression. Those who write a basically angular hand are analytical and logical. They don't merely "believe" but must be presented with all the facts. It is necessary to "convince" them, to prove "how" and "why." Being rigid, inflexible and unyielding, they prefer argument to compromise, and will seek to impose their will on others. Round writers see them as cold and inhuman, and their mechanical way of approaching life and relationships can indeed interfere with the achievement of emotional happiness. They need to cultivate tolerance, or face the disillusionment that comes when the perfect world they envision never materializes. Principles of action are often more important than results to these writers, and they will be disciplined, firm and steadfast in their convictions. Once their minds are made up, they rarely get side-tracked from an intended goal.

The angular stroke does not caress, it strikes. Hence extreme angularity accompanied by heavy pressure and pastiosity is an indication of a bad disposition with violent tendencies.

Angular writers like to figure things out and make excellent strategists, mechanics, engineers, electricians, and scientists. Their determination to succeed and ability to work energetically cannot be equalled by either the garland or the arcade type, but the variety and complexity of human emotion remains a baffling mystery to them.

ANGULAR STROKES

Generally Loopless Writers.   There are several ways of managing a loopless style of writing. The writer may choose to print rather than to connect his letters cursively, or he may proceed directly to the next letter without circling around to the left. This is called a progression, and it can be curved or an angular formation. These variations will be discussed more fully when looking at connecting strokes.

Generally speaking, loopless writers place more emphasis on the conceptual aspects of an experience than upon the emotional and feeling content of it. Here the tendency is to avoid instinctive emotional response by intellectualizing the feelings.

It's great to be here, but I wonder why I was invited. Maybe It's because I might be in -

The Stick-Figure Stroke.   Here the writer eliminates the loop in preference for the simple downstroke. It is an abbreviated stroke and indicates efficiency. Emotions are kept under control, and the writer chooses to act rather than to react. He opts for directness of approach, albeit with a certain attitude of calculation. Qualities of maturity and independence are to be found in this writer as well as the ability to make quick decisions and to eliminate unnecessary details.

the bright tongues of the flames

The Teepee Stroke. This stroke is an indication of stubbornness. These individuals take a firm stand on issues and will hold to their views even when faced with sound evidence to refute them.

I think that isn't true. Yet

The Tic. This stroke is seen as an unnecessary addition to another stroke. It indicates negative feelings of temper, anger, or hostility.

It makes me angry when you

ANGULAR SHAPES

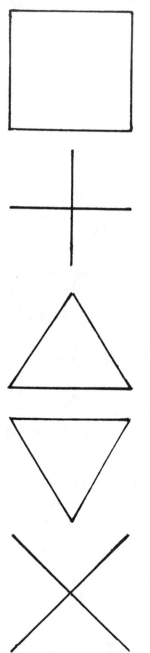

The Square provides an enclosure for defense and security. As a symbol, it indicates firmness, practicality, stability, and logic through the construction of a secure foundation. It is cold, rigid, earthbound and materialistic.

The Cross is a symbol of wisdom. It is identified with the Egyptian god Thoth—inventor of writing, the Roman god Mercury—messenger of the gods, and the Greek god Hermes—master of alchemy, the occult, and the mystical. All of these are the same god known by different names in different cultures, and each provides some form of communication through abstract means. The message can be spiritual, moralistic, idealistic or philosophic.

The Triangle stands for communication between the mental and the physical planes. It displays a logic similar to that of the square, but is more aggressive and energetic. The upward pointing triangle (movement directed to the upper zone) is considered a masculine formation and indicates a desire for recognition and achievement on a mental level. The downward pointing triangle (movement directed to the lower zone) is considered a female symbol, and here, energy is directed to experience of a physical, emotional and personal nature.

The X has been identified with death and endings. In mathematics it represents the unknown quantity. It also has religious connotations, usually Catholic or Protestant, and is a symbol of Christ and his death on the cross. Consequently, it is also a sign of martyrdom.

SQUARES, CROSSES, AND RIGHT-ANGLED SHAPES

Many squares, crosses, or right-angled shapes are an indication of materialism. These writers like possessions and the security and protection they can bring. They're earthy, practical, methodical and stubborn. It is difficult to alter their thinking with emotional pleas. They want solid evidence. They have difficulty communicating their own needs and have equal difficulty understanding the needs of others. Sometimes there is a tendency to isolation which stems from a fear of losing the self to someone else's cause. One aim in life is security through independence. Another is to avoid disappointments by avoiding relationships. These people are attracted to building, architecture, collections, securities, stocks, money, and all tangible goods.

You know — I always did like Mid West people — so direct — and I'm quite sure now. I'd like to go on vacation there. Oh, did I tell you about my new

Neither Mom or I can remember receiving a more delightful or loving thank you!

TRIANGULAR SHAPES

The Upward Pointing Triangle symbolizes the probing mind, searching for answers to sometimes inexplicable things. Emphasis is placed on qualities of reason. This type is idealistic. Once the mind is made up, decisions are stubbornly adhered to. There is mental aggression.

Molly is such a romantic. I wish she'd change. Desireing Fred as she does won't get

The Downward Pointing Triangle indicates that reason is being used to find emotional and personal meaning. The search is on, but the meaning has not been found. Feeling is something that exists without proof, and the angle wants to have the proof in hand. These people are self-critical, analytical and logical. Their approach to love is intellectual. They are often disappointed in their search for the perfect mate or in their desire for the perfect family. They are physically and emotionally aggressive.

Many things stood in the way of finding out.

The Leftward Pointing Triangle tells us that this writer is critical of his past life and relationships. There is a kind of hostility and aggression being directed to events that have already taken place. The attitude is somewhat bitter, and the writer wonders why he has been treated so unfairly. The energy is directed to reflection.

How Dare you think that of me. My family is to blame for Every

The Rightward Pointing Triangle symbolizes ambition in life and love of action. These writers are aggressive regarding their plans and goals. They are critical when others don't measure up to their conception of how the world at large should be, and are generally pessimistic in daily life.

Dear Billy, Thanks for that

X's are symbols of religion, martyrdom, endings, or death. Those who make this mark are somewhat preoccupied with rituals in their everyday life. They may not be overtly religious but do have strong beliefs. They fear death, yet have an attraction to its mystery. When the stroke is found in the lower zone the meaning is intensified. Feelings of guilt elicit strong reactions and these people can exhibit bizarre behavior. Often too, death has touched them in a personal way—such as through the death of a loved one or the death of an ideal. Sometimes they are even suicidal. They can be accident prone, attracted to drugs or alcohol, or self-destructive in other ways.

of friends. Yet we couldn't return to an urban life — Fortunately the area seems to

Middle zone and upper zone X-ing means guilt or martyrdom in daily life.

*Donald Evans
Outer View Avenue,
Los Angeles, Ca. 90001*

Lower zone X-ing indicates self-destructive tendencies.

Frankly, we are both Tired — launching the nursery

THREADED MOVEMENT

Threaded movement isn't entirely either straight or curved, but a little of each. There is more tendency to evasion than there is to action. The quality of the line is somewhat formless, and so is the quality of the character. It is a sinuous line that flattens out—giving the merest hint of the shape it's describing. It evades commitment, control and direction.

THE THREAD FORMATION

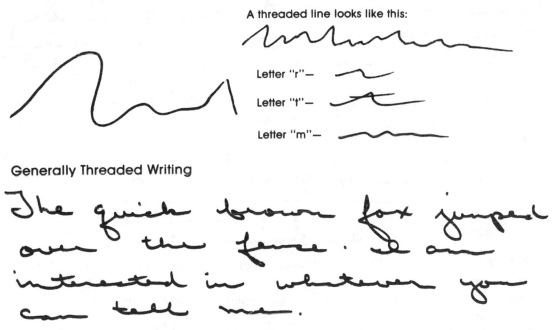

A threaded line looks like this:

Letter "r"—

Letter "t"—

Letter "m"—

Generally Threaded Writing

The quick brown fox jumped over the fence. I am interested in whatever you can tell me.

Threaded writers are sensitive and highly impressionable. They take a broad view of the world and want to see and know everything. Their innate curiosity leads them into unusual situations. Being broadminded and open to outside influences, they can be so intuitive that they actually seem to catch and hold the thoughts of others. They have a love for all the arts and want freedom to follow their own talents. Often, though, threaded writers sublimate their own creativity in order to bring it out in others. They seek appreciation rather than material rewards and consequently make good teachers and social workers.

On the negative side, threaded writers are undisciplined and unpredictable. They won't give themselves to a particular course of action, won't be pinned down, and often won't even stand up for their own convictions. The reason for this is that they are unsure about the world and unsure about themselves. They opt for an indefinite course and thus make themselves hard to understand. When they make a decision they are likely to change their minds. Dishonesty is sometimes associated with threaded writing, an association brought about by the secretive nature and formless character of the threaded writer. In any case, these people are often socially inconsiderate and eccentric in their attitudes, yet they can be the most fascinating of the four different formation types.

Often the thread formation appears as a result of speed. The mind is rushing along while the hand struggles to keep up, sacrificing legibility in the process. This fast kind of thread looks smooth and the rhythm flows, giving a uniform look to the writing. The speedy thread is identified with high intelligence—possibly even genius.

When the thready writing is not legible, the writer has difficulty communicating his intelligence.

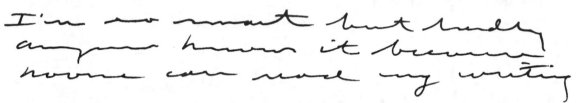

When legible, the fast-flowing thread can be an indication of true genius. These people are mentally ahead of their own time. They view the world from a wide perspective and can develop original theories.

Albert Einstein

Threading Towards the Ends of Words is a sign of the negotiator and the diplomat. These writers penetrate the thinking processes of others to see through disguises while keeping their own personality and position hidden. High intelligence is indicated.

Threading Towards the End of a Body of Writing indicates lagging interest. The writer is in a hurry to get it over with.

Threading in the Middle of Words marks the kind of indecisiveness that characterizes hysteria. These people are falling apart on the inside while maintaining a front to the outside world.

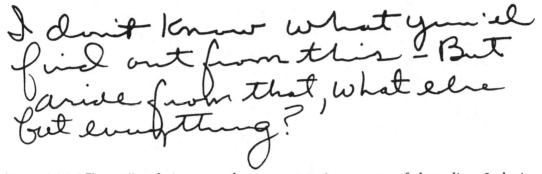

Inconsistent Threading brings out the more negative aspects of threading. Indecision, poor concentration, lack of attention to detail, evasive behavior, ambiguousness, and impressionable reactions are highlighted. Still, these writers are often the most spontaneously creative and intuitive, and can have the most original responses.

Hi Neighbor

If you want to play, you
Hoosie tomorrow and take
... doi here for the day
Then back to Devils doland.

BURT REYNOLDS,
Actor.

Sophia Loren

SOPHIA LOREN, Actress.

Robert Redford

ROBERT REDFORD, Actor.

Merry, Merry Christmas!
Olivia de Havilland

OLIVIA DE HAVILLAND, Actress.

Frank Lloyd Wright

FRANK LLOYD WRIGHT, Architect.

Please send this to Nadja
Ohanova

LEOPOLD STOKOWSKI,
Conductor.

94

Life is dangerous anyway
the bill of prints
the prints of bill

max bill

MAX BILL, Swiss artist.

MARY MARTIN, Dancer and actress.

ISAAC ASIMOV, Science fiction writer.

Dear Miss Stafford —
Is this really possible?

HENRY FONDA, Actor.

FARRAH FAWCETT, Actress.

Sincerely
Mary Pickford

RAQUEL WELCH,
Actress.

MARY PICKFORD, Actress.

TELLY SAVALAS, Actor.

LEROY JULIAN,
Adventurer.

Patriae inserviendo consumor.

PRINCE OTTO VON BISMARCK SCHONHAUSEN, German Chancellor.

Bismarck

I wonder what you will make of this

LAWRENCE OLIVIER, Actor.

GORE VIDAL, Writer.

STEVE McQUEEN, Actor.

What do you think of my Handwriting Sample today

PETER MARSHALL, Television host.

MARIE DRESSLER, Broadway entertainer.

JACK LEMMON, Actor.

RICHARD DIEBENKORN, Artist.

LEAD-IN STROKES

The stroke which begins the first letter of a word is called a lead-in stroke. These strokes, or the absence of them, give clues to the manner in which the writer relates to his family, to his own beginnings, or to the way he initiates action. The Palmer method of school copybook writing which came into use early in the 20th century taught a script style which contained lead-in strokes on most of the small letters and on some of the capitals. Most Americans have been taught this style.

A B C D E F G H I J K L M
N O P Q R S T U V W X Y Z
a b c d e f g h i j k l m n o p
q r s t u v w x y z 1 2 3 4 5 6 7 8 9 0

Secondary Lead-ins. In the Palmer Method, these strokes were attached to the small letters b, c, f, h, i, j, k, l, p, r, s, t, u, w, x, and y. On the way to maturity, many people drop the use of these strokes in favor of increased speed. Others retain them throughout life.

The presence of secondary lead-in strokes indicates adherence to patterns of behavior learned in childhood. These writers retain conventional attitudes and cling to past experiences and memories, continuing to look to authority figures and institutions for guidance. They're resistant to change, and will procrastinate a bit before entering any new project. It's as if they must warm up with a lead-in stroke before plunging into the actual letter.

overseas service group during which time
I spent a great deal of time in Africa.

Primary Lead-ins. Lead-ins attached to the letters a, c, d, g, m, n, o, and q are voluntary additions to the Palmer Method. These writers are ambitious, and put energy into life just as they do into these unlearned lead-in strokes. Still, this energy is directed into a framework of conforming values. Though opinionated and exhibitionistic, they express themselves without challenging convention or endangering their acceptance by others. They display emotion yet are deficit in inner emotional life. Decisions are delayed, spontaneity is reduced.

when you are around I feel so happy — glad to be alive and

Absence of Lead-in Strokes. This omission is an indication of maturity. These people take a direct route to problem-solving. In action, they are quick and decisive. Actual intelligence may not be higher than that found in those who retain lead-ins, but creativity and originality are more freely expressed.

When you leave, please turn out the lights.

Garland Lead-in. Warm, receptive, responsive, wants communication and acceptance. Family ties are very important. Sentimental and emotional.

The past is very important.

Long Garland Lead-in. All of the above plus good sense of humor, love of body movement, gracefully exhibitionistic.

The past is very important.

Drooping Garland Lead-in. Feels guilty, wastes time and energy, is easily led, passive, shallow thinker.

The past is very important.

Arcade Lead-in. Secretive about past and family. Proud, resistant to change, a traditionalist yet often personally eccentric. Has something to hide.

The past is very important.

Angle Lead-in. Has been hurt or cheated in the past, resents family members, is skeptical, cautious and somewhat hostile. Energy spent thinking about past.

The past is very important

Thread Lead-in. Not certain of feelings regarding past and family. Has a hard time making decisions due to conflicting impulses about past events.

The past is very important

Long Thread Lead-in. Dramatic, flirtatious, wastes others time, wants to be center of attention. Can twist the facts of family or past history.

The past is very import

Hooked Lead-in.   Can't let go of past relationships or past possessions.

The past is very important

Tics on Lead-ins.   Irritation or arrogance which is usually temporary.

The past is very important.

Lead-ins on Capitals.   Concern for appearances. Wants to hold the status-quo.

On Capitols Beautiful Dreamer

Lead-in from Below Baseline.   Negative past experiences have created aggressive feelings which result in tension and anxiety. Troubles in the teens through parents.

The past is very important.

my own fault.

With Garland Formation, person blames own self.

It's just not true

With Arcade Formation, person hides this.

all their fault.

With Angle Formation, person blames others.

Lead-ins from the Upper Zone.   Makes a show of own intelligence.

I'm very Smart — more Often

Arcade into Upper Zone.   Great imagination.

You're So Right

Angle into Upper Zone.   Probing Mind.

Mentally 1 want to know

Garland into Upper Zone.   Social intelligence.

had a broad understanding

ENDING STROKES

The stroke which ends a word is called an ending or terminal stroke. The formation of this stroke gives clues to the manner in which the writer relates to others or to his own goals.

Strong Endings of any kind.   Strong activity drives, interest in environment.

That's an ending word.

Absence of Endings. Frugality with time or money. Not dependent upon others for approval. Mental concentration, directness, self sufficiency.

That's an ending word.

Short Endings. Shyness, reticence.

That's an ending word

Long Endings. Generosity, consideration, friendliness, openness.

I'm feeling good today.

Prolonged Endings. Tenacity, extravagance, desire for conquest, mania.

I want to hold on .

Prolonged to fill space. Determination, suspicion, curiosity, tenacity, generosity, possessiveness.

I'm ready for whatcomes

Endings Up and Out. Extravagance, depends on approval, will take risks, social orientation, responsiveness, giving.

Let's go buy a new car.

Endings Up. Philosophic, seeks a higher order, ambitious, high moral standards, wants to do good works.

I want to work for a cause.

Endings Vertical. Secretive, self-conscious, in another world, imaginative, hides behind a social front.

Leave me alone.

Endings Vertical and Tight. Idealistic but not giving.

I think about things but I can't give.

Leftward Endings. Feels victimized, introverted, self-oriented, moves towards mother's world of home and protection.

Don't hurt me.

Leftward Endings under words. Self-centered, materialistic, doesn't understand others, anti-social.

I don't want to help you

Leftward endings cross through word.   Self destructive, introverted.

I hate myself.

Endings Short and Blunt.   Abrupt person, some sadistic tendencies.

I havn't time for you

Endings Thick and Clubbed.   Brutality, tenacity, sadism, great energy.

feeling cruel today

Endings Down and Weak.   Passive, timid, weak.

don't make me cry.

Endings Down and Strong.   Stubborn, tempermental, sarcastic.

Don't make me mad

Endings Down and Very Heavy.   Violence, tenacity, cruelty, determination.

Or you'll be sorry.

Endings Long and Sharp.   Hard to get along with, bad temper, sarcastic, biting personality.

Bring out the mean in

Endings Descend Vertically.   Mind is made up, intolerance, can convince others of own principles, decisive, strong likes and dislikes.

you can't change my mind.

Upturned Hook.   Keeps to traditional modes of communication, egotistic, acquisitive, steadfast.

like to talk & hang onto

Downturned Hook.   Opinionated, tenacious, materialistic, insecure.

We need to put up a new

Incomplete Endings.   Frugality, curt nature, self-sufficiency, not certain of mode of action.

as usual, I didn't know.

Dog Leg Endings.   Vanity, pretension, dishonesty, cunning.

This ending looks like this

Slurred Endings.   Dislike of detail and method, slurs over things in haste to reach goals, lack of caution. (Thread.)

come let's hurry and get

Angular Endings. Abrupt, decisive, aggressive, critical.

Let's hurry and get there

Garland Endings. Warm, responsive, talkative, social.

Let's get together soon.

Arcade Endings. Feels threatened, secretive, protective, hiding something.

don't bother me now.

Angular and Prolonged Endings. Sees life as a challenge to be met with force and discipline.

challenge to be met.

Flamboyant Endings. Immature, manic, theatrical.

Look at me.

Variety of Endings. Mixed traits—judge most prominent traits according to frequency of occurrence.

CONNECTING STROKES

Connecting strokes are those which link the letters together. They give clues to the writers social attitudes and mental abilities. In most writing you will see more than one type of connecting stroke, but some are pure examples. We'll deal with these first.

Pure Types

Garland Connectors. These people want to be needed and need to be wanted. They care what others think of them and want to come off positively. They're emotional in relationships and require a lot of attention. Communication of all kinds appeals to them—they're verbal and like to gossip. As a rule, these types are realistic, materialistic, physical, and extroverted. They're generous, flexible and expressive. Their thinking processes are usually rapid, but not particularly original.

My God, if I had known I would have to write a

Arcade Connectors. Of the two curved types, the arcade writers are more formal and controlled than their garland counterparts. They're concerned with keeping face, with traditions and with regulations. More serious than the garland, they can be just as genuinely warm, but with less ado about it. They choose their words carefully to make them more effective, and make good lecturers and teachers. They don't think as rapidly as garland writers do, but they have better memories and come to more concise conclusions. They're efficient with words and with time.

This is the way to go — Good food, Good friends — Good times I love

Angular Connectors. These writers are far more socially aggressive than the round types are. They don't particularly care whether you like them or not, and would rather argue with you than smooth things over. Generally, angular writers don't have very many friends, and are often rebellious with authority figures or superiors. They do best in their own businesses or in situations where they can deal on their terms. They're hard-working and precise, competitive and critical. These people are the most hard working of all, and also have the greatest mental potential. Angularity is a strong indication of high intelligence—usually of the scientific, logical type.

My Needs are very few. Sometimes I'm Happy and sometimes I'm Sad

Thread Connectors. These people are curious about the world around them without quite becoming involved in it. They're open and broadminded, but are inconsistent too. By the time you figure out where they stand, they stand somewhere else. They prefer interesting people to stable ones, and look for reflections of themselves in others. They're not very critical, but rather are inclined to overlook the flaws or the perfections in favor of general aspects of a person or a situation. These people are often among the most creative, but they don't follow up on this. They seek experiences rather than things, and don't want to be involved in lengthy projects.

I think the U.S.A. is wonderful and I am coming back.

Mixed Types

Garlands with Arcades. A good combination. Emotional balance—neither too receptive nor too evasive. The arch gives strength to the cup while the cup gives an expressive quality to the arch. This combination is creative and produces artists of all types. Social motivation with direct approach.

Garlands with arcades

Garlands with Angles. Another good mix. The angle gives strength to the garland and the garland provides a happier nature. The writer is observant but may not feel the need to criticize. He'd rather express in a supportive manner.

Garlands with angles

Garlands with Threads.   The mind wanders. These people have little initiative or drive. They are inclined to be lazy and lacking in will power.

Garlands with threads

Arcades with Angles.   This combination can produce a rather pompous individual. Both types are inclined to be perfectionistic, and will rise to the top professionally, but the emotional life is undeveloped. These people are stubborn and inflexible and extremely critical. Their lack of tolerance can drive loved ones away.

Arcades with angles

Arcades with Threads.   An extremely creative combination. These people are little understood by friends and associates. There is a great deal beneath the surface as both types tend to be secretive. Often this mixture can produce the criminal mind. The thread urges the arcade to do those bizarre things he's always thinking about. Without garlands to provide guilt, these people could become actively antisocial.

Arcades with threads

Angles with Threads.   Sometimes this is a brilliant combination. The directness and aggressive force of the angle can stimulate the thread to action. The openminded attitudes of the thread can modify the demanding nature of the angle. The angle is usually the most intelligent while the thread is the most open to stimulation and experience. Each provides what the other is missing.

Angle with thread

Progressions.   This is another type of connecting stroke. It proceeds directly from one letter to the next without returning to the baseline or making a loop on the letter.

Curved Progressions Formed with Garlands.   Here the writer is making a gesture of friendship and response without going out on an emotional limb. Give and take attitudes with dependency are emphasized.

Curved Progressions Formed with Arcades.   These formations emphasize mental and theatrical orientation. The writer makes a show of his knowledge and behaves in a defensive or protective manner regarding emotional feelings.

Angular Progressions.   These formations emphasize mental concepts. This writer analyzes and probes, seeking to find the meaning of a situation.

this ghost · This ghost · this ghost

Garland   Arcade   Angle

Connectedness and Disconnectedness

The child who is learning to write first learns each letter separately and only gradually learns to connect them to form one continuous word. In the maturation process, as writing becomes automatic, the ability to connect groups of letters is attained. The longer the sequence of joined letters, the higher the degree of connectedness.

Comparative studies of speech and writing have confirmed the close correlation between these two language functions. Those who write a smooth connected hand can speak with fluency. Those with speech defects mirror these in their writing.

Writing speed is greater with connected forms because connecting letters facilitates the writing process. Even writers who ordinarily disconnect many letters write with a higher degree of connectedness when circumstances force them to write faster than their normal pace.

Although the Palmer Method teaches a totally connected (cursive) writing style, the average adult makes some changes as he matures, and it isn't uncommon to pause in the writing sequence to cross t's, dot i's or indicate syllables.

The degree of connectedness present in a sample gives clues to the writer's thinking processes, mental abilities, and social attitudes.

CONNECTED WRITING

When most of the letters in a body of writing are connected, the writing is termed "connected." There are varying degrees of connectedness. Generally speaking, connected writers are logical, rational and analytical. Their thinking is systematic, and their sense of calculation and strategy moves them to want to plan ahead. They are goal-minded and are persistent and purposeful. They are able to sort out facts comprehensively, organize them into cohesive wholes and come to definite conclusions. These writers are determined, practical and realistic. They want reasons for everything. They like to start projects at the beginning and proceed chronologically to the conclusion. Once started on a task, they don't like to be interrupted until they've arrived at a proper stopping point. Great power of concentration enables them to think, plan, act and execute according to their preconceived ideas. Connected writers want to bring things together, arrange them into proper order and deliver them systematically.

Negatively, connected writers can sometimes get so caught up in the details and their order that they miss the overall pattern of meaning. They may be intuitive, but they won't go with the feeling until they've completely dissected and analyzed it. They want to be sure there's a reason for feeling the way they do before acting on the feeling.

Connected writers are restless. They seek and desire change. If their minds aren't continually stimulated, they get bored. It's hard for them to sit and stare into space. A mental challenge is often more relaxing than doing nothing. They're fond of crossword puzzles and other games.

Socially, these writers can be inconsiderate and tactless. It's not that they mean to be, it's just that when they finally come up with the answer to someone's problem as they see it, they're not above saying it like it is. They're often much better at solving abstract problems than personal ones, as the closer they are to something the less able they are to see it clearly. They're so busy thinking about what has already happened or what will happen next that they miss what is happening now.

These connected types are fond of reading and study. They make good students and have very good memories for facts—clear back to childhood, but it's hard for them to remember some of their daily-life obligations, and to avoid embarrassment, it becomes necessary to write appointments down.

Boy are I tired. I just finished final exams for the second year.

Extreme Connectedness.   Although this was the way most of us learned to connect in the Palmer Method, retention of extreme connectedness into adulthood is an indication of compulsive tendencies. This type behaves automatically in social situations. He has a hard time bringing his feelings to the surface where they can be communicated, yet since the connected writer is communicative by nature, he'll relate through a symbolic or ritualistic act if he can't express verbally. The general qualities of connectedness are found magnified in this type, but slavish adherence to copybook connecting indicates blocks to the expression of more creative or unusual ideas and abilities. Here, the mind tends to focus on the objective to such an extent that receptivity to change or readiness to accept new opportunities or developments spontaneously is impossible. This writer limits himself.

I think it would be fun to leave my fling but can't or won't just

Connections Between Words.   When writing is so connected that not only letters but even words are linked together, it is an indication of great concentration. These writers do everything according to preconceived plans, from the first thought to the completion of the act. This trait is rare, but is found in the writings of various strategists. Where there is a link between the words while some breaks occur within them, an avant-garde type of creativity and originality is indicated. These writers are not bound by convention. In some cases, when the rest of the writing is not particularly harmonious or well-integrated, this unusual connectedness indicates flightiness of ideas and an inability to focus on the real issues.

My idea is that we have someone who can deliver the goods at the proper time and place. After all, we should try to get it over with early so we can get back to

you know that I wanted it that way when we first spoke about it by telephone

Partial Connectedness.   Many adult writers pause periodically to dot i's, cross t's, move to a next syllable or think about what comes next. Sometimes too, even though the motion of the hand is smooth and continuous, the hand will lift just enough to leave the paper for an instant. Any of these things can be done without disrupting the flow of the writing. These people possess the qualities of the connected writer, but are not so single-minded, focused, or compulsive as the totally connected types are. There is more spontaneity expressed which allows for the development of creative potential. Some of the qualities of the disconnected writer are incorporated with the traits of the connected type to produce a broader individual who hopefully has the best of both worlds.

Warning. The surgeon general has determined that cigarette smoking may be hazardous

DISCONNECTED WRITING

When the strokes which ordinarily link the letters are nearly or totally absent the writing is termed "disconnected." The fewer the connecting strokes, the more disconnected is the writing.

Constant interruption of the writing movement with stops and starts between letters wastes time and energy. With increased speed requirements, even very disconnected writing or printing contains more connecting strokes than usual. The trend to connectedness increases with speed and decreases when the forms are slowly and carefully traced.

Generally speaking, disconnected writers are open to the influence of the moment. They have a hard time filtering out unnecessary or unwanted stimulation. Emotional sensitivity and perception are so heightened that groups of people overstimulate them, and for self-protective purposes, they generally adopt an almost hermetic life-style. Personally, they are egocentric, inconsistent, moody, restless, shy, unsociable, selfish, cautious, fearful, unadaptable, lonely, and insecure. All of these traits might be considered negative, but keep in mind that these people need to maintain a certain amount of psychic distance for their own preservation.

The main thing about the mental inclinations of disconnected writers is that their opinions come from a sense of feeling rather than from reasoning. Certain inner convictions exist independently of logic and these are relied upon. Their ideas are very personal and sometimes greatly inventive. They know without knowing they know; sometimes this intrinsic knowledge shows the inspiration of genius, while in other cases it is simply a spastic kind of thinking process that leads nowhere. These people think in whole concepts rather than in a systematic order. They have a good memory for impressions and are extremely observant. More speculative and original than connected types, they have great imaginative potential, quick grasp and insight, independence of judgement, inventive and inspirational thoughts, critical ability, good sense of timing, and individualism. Negatively, disconnected writers have a lack of ability to see themselves critically, are impractical, unreasonable and unorganized. They form strong likes and dislikes on the basis of first impressions and appearances. These instantaneous reactions are often emotional, and, if uncontrolled, are intensified by the senses so strongly that violent outbursts can result. Their reactions are instinctive in contrast to the connected types who calculate their actions.

high degree to reveal or define the major aspects of a personality, but have reservations about accepting it as the final answer in getting to know another person, people being

Totally Disconnected Cursive Writing. If you consider the sideways movement of connecting strokes as links between the ego and the outside world, it becomes clear that total lack of connectedness is a serious defect. These people have difficulty understanding relationships or adapting their behavior to suit the situation. It's hard for them to link their experiences into a meaningful direction. This leads to introversion, social withdrawal or isolation. The desire to absorb rather than to express or communicate makes these types stingy with social overtures.

I'm not sure what to write about Probably I'm incriminating myself already. Oh well, here goes.

Disconnected, Detached and Original Printing. This is a highly creative category. These writers are inspired, individualistic, and likely to work in an artistic field. They size people and situations up quickly and then jump to conclusions.

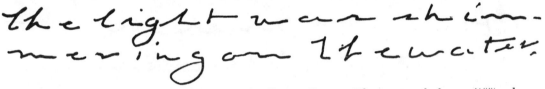

the light was shimmering on the water.

Full Disconnections with Hesitancy in the Formations. These people have difficulty translating their thoughts to words or their goals to action.

He said he would be busy until about

Printed Writing. A higher percentage of left-handers adopt printing as their mode of writing than do right-handers. In both instances, these people may have had trouble learning to write, and as soon as possible, dropped writing in favor of printing. Qualities of introversion and competitiveness combine to produce personalities who would rather not participate at all unless they can play to win. Printers feel rebellious toward traditional social situations and toward ties that bind. They're individualists, hermits, or anti-social neurotics. They're full of feelings of inadequacy and isolation, but won't admit to the emptiness they experience. They strive for perfection in all things and do not wish to become personally involved with others to any great extent. They're self-centered and lonely—critical and aloof. They'd rather do things alone than cooperate with others and have difficulty identifying with causes or goals.

There is a possible short trip on the horizon. My plans are still the same regarding the new

Aesthetic Printing.   The print-style of some designers and engineers is frequently constructed to attain physical beauty or for the goal of precision and legibility. Qualities of appearance are more important to these people than social connections are, and they may or may not be intuitive or introverted. Other qualities in the writing will help you decide.

You'll uncover a wealth of information. It's simple. It's fun. With amazing speed and

Printed Word or Phrase in a Cursive Writing.   The writer wants to be personally removed from or unconnected with the particular name, word, or phrase he has printed. He may be lying or may feel threatened.

On Friday we went on down to the CHURCH, and when I think you should speak to your father about that.

Sporadic Alternation Between Printing and Writing.   This indicates confusion about social roles, inconsistency in thinking processes, or changes in modes of expression. This is a strong indication of mental or emotional instability.

The men were willing to go along with it, but then all of a sudden I had the feeling that it really wouldn't be a very good idea after all, so I tried to

Printing with All Capital Letters.   This is much the same as writing with an over-developed middle zone and is an indication of self-centeredness, insensitivity to feeling and experience, and focus on daily-life activities. Feelings of guilt block channels of self-development. The writer may be quite sophisticated and immature at the same time.

I've always wondered if the fact that I print instead of write make it impossible to analyze my personality.

PATRICIA NIXON, Wife of President Richard Nixon.

their precious friendship is a priceless gift!
With appreciation and Happy New Year wishes,
As always,
Pat Nixon

thank Mr Shepherd for his kindness of about the Eric beds; Mildred & of the family are here as usual. in Cousin. R E Lee

ROBERT E. LEE, Confederate General during the Civil War.

will be saved from the soul-destroying immorality of our nation.
May God Bless you!
Anita Bryant Green
Phil. 4:13

ANITA BRYANT, Singer and anti-homosexual rights crusader.

Archibald Cox

ARCHIBALD COX, Attorney and Special Prosecutor, Nixon Administration.

joyous, and stars shine in the dark that cannot be seen by day
Cordially
Helen Keller.

HELEN KELLER, Famous blind deaf-mute, who became an outstanding personality.

Things may have been
hectic in '77, but
we both know they're
changing for the better
in '78.

Love

Vikki

VIKKI CARR, Singer.

ELLIOT RICHARDSON,
Attorney General,
Nixon Administration.

Eunice K. Shriver

EUNICE KENNEDY SHRIVER,
Sister of President John Kennedy.

If I prefer to hear from you again, if it is not asking too much,
I return the copy, not only so that I may gain time
so that I may have the benefit of your further advice.
Yours by right of discovery
R. L. Frost.

ROBERT FROST, Poet, age 20.

Sorry so late with.
This, I had to leave
town suddenly
Again thanks

VINCENT PRICE,
Actor.

Dear Mr.

Thank you so very much for your letter — I did appreciate hearing

JACQUELINE KENNEDY,
Wife of President John Kennedy.

*for you — ask what you can do
for your country — my fellow
citizens of the world. ask not
or others
what America will do for you —
but rather what you can do*

JOHN KENNEDY,
American President.

*I must tell you about Chamber Music
at Mrs Johnson's. It was the most agonizing
experience of my life. Mrs J told us to arrive
at 10:30. "Oh good" said Jackie, "That means
the concert and a fabulous souper afterwards."*

LEE RADZIWILL,
Sister of Jacqueline
Kennedy.
Sample written
when a teenager.

*Monsieur le Duc de
Chartres
à Chartres*

26 juin 1760

MADAME DE
POMPADOUR,
Mistress of
Louis XV
of France.

*bonjour mon cochon, vous avez bien raison
et je dis plus que jamais ah qu'il*

Self-Image Concepts

THE PERSONAL PRONOUN "I"

The personal pronoun I has great importance in that it is symbolic of the writer himself. The formation of this single letter reveals the person's ego, that is, his self-image and his sense of his own worth. It also gives clues to the regard in which he wishes to be held by others. And, by studying the personal pronoun I, the degree and the quality of influence that the mother and father figures have had in shaping the writer's personality can be determined.

Normally the space taken for the personal pronoun I is similar to other capital letters in the handwriting. Extreme ego height as found in a very tall or very inflated I or the opposite extreme of ego shrinking as seen in tiny or crushed forms are both aspects of the same thing, self-concern.

Just as with the body of the writing, the more natural or average the slant of the personal pronoun I, the more freely and flexibly the writer will respond to others and his own life situations. Left-tending I's are not easily written by the right hand and tend therefore to be more artificial; the writer is covering an inner reserve, defensiveness, or rebellion with carefully practiced outer behavior. Genuine forward movement is repressed and inner caution prevails. Often there is a strong tie to the mother figure.

Those who write a vertical personal pronoun I value their independence and wish to find their own way in life. These people have the will power to block out emotional distractions and value harmony and privacy. They respond to life but at the same time will protect their innermost feelings.

When the personal pronoun I leans to the left and the balance of the writing moves rightward expect inner neurosis, personal disharmony and conflict. Here is the lack of insight and empathy associated with the back-slanted I combined with the will to move out and impress the environment. The person is isolated within his self-involvement in spite of his activity.

Take special note of the writer who reverses the writing direction of the I; in superior writings he could be a genius as he is asserting a private need for originality. Generally, however, a reversal is covert defiance. The writer is privately having his own way, and will do the opposite of what is expected of him.

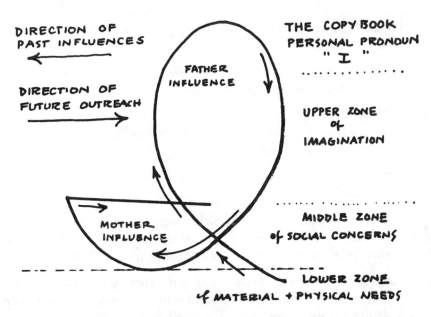

Looking at the male and female aspects of the personal pronoun I, it is to be expected that the greater the emphasis upon the upper or father-oriented portion of the letter, the stronger the desire of the writer to relate to that image. The longer or more emphasized the female zone, the stronger the ties are there. Sharp points or angles in these areas indicate hostility toward that figure, just as retracing indicates repressed or unacknowledged feeling toward the mother or father, usually painful feeling.

When the I is printed or written as a single straight line the self may be viewed as standing alone without encumbering or immature ties to either parent figure, or indeed without troubling need for emotional support concerning the self-image.

Certain elaborated or overly embellished versions of the I are done to reassure the writer and to impress others that things are better than they really are. Such a person usually possesses little insight about himself, is interested in being considered creative, and is prone to waste time because of his need to release tension through imagination or fantasy.

Some I shapes are so malformed as to appear twisted and ill. Such an ego may indeed be deformed, or a physical problem will reveal itself in the body of the writing that influences the ego symbol. Clues to the personality also turn up in personal pronoun I's that are shaped like dollar signs, circles, cradles, knots, daggers, or a number, like 2. In this fashion the I constitutes a word in itself, a drawing of the ego.

SPECIFICS OF THE PERSONAL PRONOUN I

I   **Printed in Cursive Writing** . . . clear constructive thinking . . . independent . . . desire to stand out.

Stick Figure . . . very independent . . . culturally aware and mature . . . lack of facade.

Lower Case Letter . . . either a crushed or totally immature ego, or a conscious desire to draw attention to self.

Tall Inflated Upper loop . . . a vain person, whose vanity can quickly disappear under adversity . . . outgoing and enjoys spotlight . . . imagination . . . wishful thinking.

Tall Narrow Upper Loop . . . must be in command to feel worthwhile . . . lofty idealism . . . often unrealistic.

Retraced Loops . . . repressed feelings about self and others, lack of spontaneity and confidence . . . conservative . . . if left-slanted, needs protection and comfort . . . lacks insight into self and others.

Upper Loop without Base . . . identification with father or male role, denial of mother . . . idealism and ethical principles are important . . . self-protective . . . influenced by early life experience.

Open Reclined Cradle . . . overly involved with mother figure, which can be hostile dependence . . . cannot assert self or say no . . . hates conflict . . . vulnerable to male dominance.

Extra Loop on Reclined Cradle . . . strong child-like attachment to maternal figure.

Arrow to the Left . . . hostility or bitterness toward the mother figure.

Arrow on Upper Loop . . . anger or disappointment toward the father figure . . . self-criticism . . . judgemental.

Circle or Arcaded . . . protective of self with limited self-understanding . . . need for mothering.

Knotted . . . self-centered and ungiving . . . self-protective . . . emotional in a shallow or showy manner . . . a "butterfly".

Upper and Lower Endings Rightward . . . resents imagined impositions . . . tends to blame others when things go wrong . . . very limited insight into self or others.

Springboard or Pedestal Stroke . . . the lower zone drives are the source of personal motivation . . . can be stubborn and prejudiced.

Number Two Shape . . . writer has felt second-class either physically or emotionally, or both, and has learned to shield emotions . . . overcompensates with an acute sense of independence . . . will not relate intimately.

Dollar Sign . . . ego involvement with money as a source of personal value; possibly "bought off" as a child with $ instead of love . . . also can be a crossing out of self if strokes angled or scribbled; this highly neurotic.

X-Ing . . . strong fears and dependency.

Coiling . . . self-conscious . . . pretentious . . . eccentric.

Distortion . . . physical illness or deformity . . . self-conscious desire to be noticed . . . prefers the unusual or romantic to reality . . . rebellion . . . struggle with self-image

Backward or Reversed Formation . . . Any letter written in a direction opposite to that which was taught implies rebellion to some degree on the part of the writer; in high quality handwritings this reversal can be an expression of genius. In the personal pronoun I the reversed direction usually indicates talent impaired by neurosis. The writer will be perverse, will do the opposite of what is expected of him, resents authority, and might even come to grips with the law.

In the reversed personal pronoun I, since the bottom is formed first there is usually indication of an abnormal affiliation with the mother figure. The ego has not completely separated from the mother, or mother substitute, and clings if only to thwart her.

THE SMALL LETTER d

Always notice the small letter "d." Like the personal pronoun I, it is especially revealing of the ego traits and the social attitudes of the writer. The d, however, tells us more about how the individual can be expected to interact socially with other people, whereas the personal pronoun I showed us the person's internalized social and self image.

General rules of slant and size apply to the d as to all letters. However, there are certain changes in the d letter shape and in the stem of the d that give clues to personal traits like vanity, independence, vulnerability, even the possibility of maniacal behavior. The letter specifics below are the best way to study this important letter.

Stem High and Retraced . . . quiet pride and dignity . . . independent . . . will not show hurt feelings.

Stem Low and Retraced . . .shrewd . . . independent . . . modest good judgement; when too short, a crushed social ego.

Stem Makes Wide Loop . . . the bigger the loop the more sensitive the person . . . touchy and vulnerable to both criticism and flattery.

Stem Makes Tall Wide Loop . . . vanity, conceit, and arrogance . . . hyper-sensitive to criticism.

Stem Makes Tall Wide Loop with Point at Top . . . same as above but with feelings of being alone and different . . . often immature and neurotic about self-image.

Greek d . . . love of and concern for culture . . . poetic and literary abilities . . . emphasis upon reason and excellence, mature social abilities.

Teepee d . . . obstinacy and stubbornness, particularly in social situations . . . reticence.

Open d . . .like the oval letters, a's and o's, in the tendency to be voluble, chatty, to talk a lot . . . these letters are like open mouths.

Pedestal d . . . obstinant, stubborn, and unyielding . . . a desire to control situations . . . firm convictions and strong prejudices.

Stem Makes Rightward Flag . . . flirtatious, gay, socially aggressive . . . fun-loving . . . pleasure-oriented.

Embellished Stem . . . pretentiousness . . . eccentricity.

Lasso Loop Stem . . . child-like, naive nature . . . sometimes a poetic nature.

Felon's Claw Formation . . . a person who habitually provokes others . . . self-punishing . . . impossible to get along with for any length of time.

Backward or Reversed Formation . . . social conflict with authority . . . contrariness or outright rebellion . . . amorality . . . criminal behavior . . . can show sexual inversion such as homosexuality, latent or overt.

Inflated into Lower Zone . . . unconscious fixation upon the mother figure . . . the same as a left-tending y loop.

Circle Stem . . . a magic circle that protects deep neurotic fearfulness in social situations . . . hidden anti-social impulses . . . self-protective.

Spiral Stem . . . egocentricity . . . emotional selfishness . . . a narcissist who loves himself too much to care for another.

Cracked Stem . . . extreme touchiness . . . neurotic social adjustment to the environment.

Maniac d . . . person given to sudden emotional outbursts or extreme emotional reactions . . . one of the signs of a criminal nature.

T-BARS: WILL POWER, ACTIVE OR PASSIVE *t*

Many handwriting analysts consider the letter "t" by far the most graphologically important letter of the alphabet. In order to make a t-bar the writer interrupts the normal up, down, and circular movements of his hand to produce a separate and distinct line. Unconsciously this requires a slight added attention and exertion. How the writer draws this bar tells how will power and personal drive are expressed in his life.

Will, or directed energy, supplies the drive necessary to overcome constant everyday obstacles and to achieve an inner discipline; its quality is vital to the harmony of the personality. In a person's handwriting the length, pressure, placement, and shape of the t crossing reveal the rhythm and force of the will behind. Be aware of a mixture of t-bars, which indicates conflicting goals and confusion in thought and action.

Furthermore, the placement of the t-bar on the stem is a major clue to the individual's goals; are they average, high, totally unrealistic? There must be over fifty different ways to cross a t, and a writer will often change or modify his style as his personality changes, or his health alters. The most common examples are defined below.

Length of t Crossing:
Short Crossing . . . lack of drive and will power . . . in superior scripts, reserve and restraint of natural instincts, in inferior script, lack of confidence, timidity.

Average Crossing . . . healthy balance, calmness, self-control in thought and action.

Long Crossing . . . energy, vigor, resolution, boldness . . . an overly-long crossing not only implies the same confidence, persistence and enthusiasm, but also a person consumed with ambition who cannot be stopped.

Pressure of t Crossing:
Pressure Lighter than Stem . . . resignation . . . extreme sensitivity . . . timidity.

Pressure Heavier than Stem . . . domineering will and great energy, but capable of insensitivity and selfishness in pursuing goals.

Starts Thick and Ends Thin . . . quick-witted and sarcastic.

Starts Thin and Ends Thick . . . the club shape that means cruelty and possible brutality.

Angle of t Crossing:
Ascending . . . optimism, ardor, enthusiasm, ambition.

Descending with Light Pressure . . . like x-ing, dependency, fear, and hopeless resignation.

Descending with Heavy Pressure . . . stubborness and an argumentative nature . . . very heavy pressure leads to despotism, aggressiveness, destructiveness, and cruelty.

Position of the t Crossing:
Low, Medium, and High on Stem . . . the individual's goals will be of corresponding importance to him.

High Above Stem . . . imagination and leadership in superior script but prejudice in lesser scripts . . . goals not realistic but are founded in fantasy and imagination . . . found in women who marry for wealth or importance. . . also found in those with love of physical adventure.

Crossing to Left of Stem . . . procrastination, indecisiveness.

Crossing to Right of Stem . . . impulsiveness, enthusiasm, animation, nervous energy.

No Crossing . . . haste and carelessness . . . absent-mindedness . . . despondency . . . rebelliousness.

Shape of t Crossing:
Hooks on t-Bar . . . persistence and tenacity of purpose . . . hooks at each end show a compulsive and indomitable nature that can drive the person to exhaustion even in tasks of little value.

Bowed Bar High on Stem . . . a nature in which strong passions and appetites have been subdued, often through spiritual values . . . can be inhibition, or protective umbrella.

Inverted Bow . . . instability, fickleness, shallow interests, someone easily influenced with a weak avoidance of confrontations . . . willfulness . . . indulgence of sensual appetites . . . guilt-ridden desire to be victim.

Wavy Bar . . . fast and intuitive mind . . . fanciful humor . . . good nature and gaiety . . . gracious and sociable.

Looped or Knotted Bar . . . persistence and tenacity, a person who rarely gives up . . . great concentration . . . logical and materialistic.

Star-Shaped Knot . . . hard angles without lifting the pen show not just persistence but an angry obstinacy . . . the star-shape with a weak bar not passing through the stem shows procrastination and indecision coupled with repression . . . the star-shape with a strong bar off the stem: indomitable.

Leftward Return Stroke . . . desire to protect self, often to point of selfishness . . . lack of confidence . . . introversion and return to past . . . jealousy.

Whip Shape t Bar . . . practical joker . . . show-off . . . mimic.

Shape of t Stem
Loop with No Bar . . . usually occurring at the end of a word; hypersensitivity and deep emotions but without the discipline of reason.

Retraced Stem with No Bar . . . usually occurring at the end of a word; speed and efficiency when other t-crossings present, making it an acceptable variation of the Palmer style.

Looped Stem with Crossing . . . imagination . . . writer needs considerable support from those around him.

Splinting or Double-Stroke Stem . . . writer falls into the neurotic category with conflict between what the mind dictates and what the emotions demand. . . overly fearful and suspicious.

Cracked or Spiral Stem . . . a neurotic person with difficulty in making adjustments to life . . . odd and eccentric . . . self-involved.

THE I-DOT

The meaning of the formation and placement of the small letter i-dot is very similar to that of the variations of the t-bar. Dotting the i is also an interruption of the forward movement of the writing, and only the slow, careful hand makes it precisely round and places it exactly over the i. More often we find dots wandering forward or backward, up or down, or turning into hasty dashes.

Like the t-bar, the location of the i-dot in the upper zone relates it to the intellect and the aspirations. High or low, it tells us of enthusiasm or practicality. The more strangely the i-dot is made, the farther the person will be removed from the commonplace. In cases where the i is not dotted (in such instances we are likely to find many uncrossed t's as well), we have an indication of carelessness, poor memory, or on a deeper level, blind spots in the thinking or depression.

Round and Placed Over the Stem . . . order, method, precision . . . conscientiousness . . . good memory and concentration.

Round and Placed High Above the Stem . . . great imagination and enthusiasm . . . if very light, spirituality.

Very Low . . . constraint . . . caution . . . fear . . . illness.

Omitted . . . carelessness . . . absent-mindedness . . . lack of mental orderliness . . . poor memory . . . blind spots . . . depression.

Muddy and Blotched . . . materialism . . . sensualism . . . sensuous appreciation of sounds and colors.

Very Light . . . sensitive . . . frail . . . unassertive.

Very Dark . . . emphatic . . . assertive . . . overbearing.

Placed After the Stem . . . impatience . . . impulsiveness . . . in good scripts, a quick mind that looks ahead.

Placed Before the Stem . . . procrastination . . . timidity . . . caution and fear of new ideas.

A Sharp Accent . . . lively wit . . . original mind . . . if high and dashed, vivacity and imagination.

A Sharp Accent Reversed and the Tent Shape . . . good critical sense and intellectual abilities.

Arrow Shape . . . cruelty and sarcasm.

Club Shape . . . cruelty and irritability . . . domineering . . . if very heavy, pugnacity.

Curved or Crescent Shaped or Wavy . . . sense of humor . . . vivacity . . . love of fun.

Dot Joined to the Following Letter . . . activity, a mind that works much faster than the hand and does not want to lose its train of thought.

Circle I-Dot . . . interest in arts and crafts, manually dextrous, a feeling for design in fields of adaptive or interpretive art rather than original fine art . . . in inferior script can be a sign of emotional instability, or a person who wishes to appear different and "arty" but is basically merely faddish or highly narcissistic.

In a man's script the circle i-dot is a feminine trait that points to insecurity over the masculine image and sexual immaturity. His interests are characteristically feminine, such as fashion, dancing, cosmetics and hair-styling.

Yours very truly
Alfred Nobel

ALFRED NOBEL,
Industrialist and
philanthropist.

Sally Rand

SALLY RAND,
Fan dancer.

L. RON HUBBARD,
Religious leader.

GENERAL WESTMORELAND
Military officer.

Diahann Carroll

DIAHANN CARROLL, Singer.

I think I've always been a
Mime — My family tells me that
I never spoke a single word until
I was age four. It always

30 YEAR OLD MIME, Performer.

WALTER WRISTON,
Bank president.

Foreword
Franklin D. Roosevelt
March 11 — 1941

FRANKLIN D. ROOSEVELT,
President.

...nisally, I am a bit apprehensive about
... or not my handwriting, should be
be analyzed to give an insight into
"why" and "how" of my life. But

Writer of musical shows.

123

I am walking down the street to get the horse & carriage out of the old garage.

LINUS PAULING,
Scientist.

ARNIE LEVIN, Artist.

MERLE OBERON,
Actress.

WALT DISNEY, Artist.

U.S.S.

JOHN TUNNEY,
U.S. Senator.

IGOR STRAVINSKY, Musician.

RICHARD NIXON FAMILY

124

Mr Lindbergh only wasting
time with his search

BRUNO HAUPTMAN,
Kidnap-murderer.

This is probably typical of
my serious handwritings!

KARL MENINGER,
Psychiatrist.

Karl Menninger MD

Lovingly ever thine MBEddy

Pleasant View.
Concord NH Oct. 3 1904

Leibniz

LIEBNIZ,
Scientist.

My dearest Student
I sent
to you a 20 dollar
gold piece not
as money, for that
can neither express
nor pay for yours

Franz Kafka

FRANZ KAFKA,
Author.

MARY BAKER EDDY, Religious leader.

Mozart

MOZART, Musician.

Lady Bird Johnson

Luci Johnson Nugent   *Lynda Johnson Robb*

LYNDON JOHNSON FAMILY

125

Signatures

The signature and the personal pronoun I are probably the two most intimate graphic movements that a person makes on the paper. They are representations of the self, self-image concepts condensed into a small but telling format. However, where the personal pronoun I tells the graphologist what the writer secretly thinks of himself, the signature is a conscious form of handwriting.

Although a signature can develop naturally as the person matures, as often as not it is produced by practice to see whether we "like" it, or it is destroyed by use as happens to some doctors or directors of corporations who must sign thousands of stock certificates. This conscious form of handwriting, which is accepted as a representation of the self on checks, credit cards, driver's licences, and documents, represents our own idea of ourselves and how we hope others will see us. It is the public self, on view for all to see.

Analyzing a signature by itself rarely can give a complete picture of the writer; more often than not, the signature will differ from the main body of writing, making a comparison of the two very important. When the signature is legible and shows no difference from a legible script, it follows that the writer will be a natural and unselfconscious person who will behave alike in public and private. Now consider the meanings of the variations possible between the signature and the styles of the script:

Signature Smaller than the Script. The writer is more modest than he demonstrates. He is assuming a mild, forceless, rather servile role in life, and is likely to put himself down. Occasionally this can be a protective measure on the part of an over-sensitive, introverted, or shy person.

Signature Larger than the Script.   The writer is advertising, and wishes to be recognized as an important person. Pride, self-esteem, ambition, self-confidence are shown, and in overly large signatures these qualities take on the character of false pride, pretentiousness, a driving need to call attention to the self. In bloated weak formations this is a false front.

Signature Slants Left with a Rightward Script.   This combination is rare and often temporary. A sort of brake is being applied to the natural responsiveness; a reserve and restraint has been erected toward the public. There is more reserve and control in the character structure than anyone would expect.

Signature Slants Right with a Vertical or Leftward Script. Here the writer is presenting a warm and out-going front to the world, but this is actually the cultivated act of a basically aloof and private personality. Since balance in acting is difficult to achieve, particularly on a daily basis, these people are often very demonstrative and effusive, overdoing their inner reserve with a sort of instant intimacy. If clever, these introverts with the public personalities can carry out schemes of a secretive nature.

Vertical Signature with Upright or Left Inclined Script. This writer will appear poised, in command of himself, and often very charming in public. His ability to see himself and consider his actions makes interpersonal relationships smooth for him. The degree of intimacy of which he is capable on a personal basis depends upon the spacing and slant of the script, the leftward or reclined script always denoting caution.

Placement of the Signature on the Page:
Signature placed at the left of the page shows a writer clinging to the past, afraid of moving forward into the future. There is inhibition and lack of confidence. An exception to this is the writer influenced by contemporary business usage which has promoted left placement as being quicker to type. Like all typed business forms this position sometimes finds its way into personal style.
Signature placed at the center of the page indicates a person who likes to be in the center of things. If the signature is large he wishes to be the center of attention and to dominate. Actors and actresses often sign like this.
Signature placed at the right of the page is that of a person moving comfortably with life. Too far to the right or running off the page suggests extreme impulsiveness and fanaticism.

Legibility of the Signature:
Illegible writing with a legible signature is unusual in its extreme egocentricity. Rarely does a person write in such a way as not to communicate his thoughts but only his name. Mental disturbance or immaturity could cause this.
Legible writing with an illegible signature communicates the writer's thoughts but not his identity. Depending upon the size and formation of the signature he could be very secretive, creative, impatient, inwardly hateful of himself, or could have reduced his name to a hieroglyph like a doctor or an artist sometimes does over the years.
Illegible writing with an illegible signature in a script of poor rhythm and form quality indicates drugs or mental illness. Otherwise it is a thoroughly egocentric and impatient person who simply doesn't care whether he can be read or not. Underneath these people are often unstable and lonely, and sometimes resort to printing in block letters to be a part of the world.
A portion of the signature reduced in size, crossed out by another stroke, or written illegibly shows the writer's hostility to just that portion of his name. Occasionally the entire signature is circled protectively or crossed out angrily with slash-ing t-bars and endings. Such x-ing shows self-directed anger and is one of the signs of suicidal tendencies.

BILL HAYES,
Actor.

ROMAN POLANSKI,
Movie director.

LOWELL THOMAS, Travel author.

GAMAL ABDUL NASSER,
Egyptian President.

CHARLES DICKENS,
Writer.

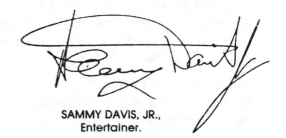

BENJAMIN FRANKLIN,
Statesman.

ANN LANDERS, Columnist.

SAMMY DAVIS, JR.,
Entertainer.

Overscoring and Underscoring. The stroke underlining the name, whatever its quality, shows self-confidence and ego emphasis. Judged by its clarity and elaboration it shows the degree of pride and self-confidence. The overscore signifies selfishness, and self-protectivensss. Framed by an overscore and underscore both, the signature shows great egocentrism as well as inner reserve, mistrust and selfishness.

Large Capitals. Elevated and inflated first letters imply extreme pride (unless the personal pronoun I is small, in which case the writer is compensating for inferiority feelings). Such a writer wants to achieve a prominent public place in life. Very unusual large capitals are a projection of inner fantasy life, repressed wishes.

The graphic imagery of the **Creative Signature** will mirror or express the nature of the creative drive, as in the beat of music, the stroke of brush or pen, or creative imagery that reflects the professional involvement.

SIGNATURES WHICH REFLECT
PRIDE AND TRADITION
CREATIVITY . . .
OSTENTATION . . .

ANDREW YOUNG: Former U.S. Delegate, U.N.

WILBUR MILLS,
U.S. Senator.

GEORGE McGOVERN,
Politician.

PIERRE TRUDEAU, Canadian Prime Minister.

ED MUSKIE,
Politician.

JAMES M. GAVIN,
Actor.

O. J. SIMPSON, Athlete.

JOHN WAYNE, Actor.

LAWRENCE WELK, Musician.

JOHN GIELGUD, Actor.

Below: NELSON A. ROCKEFELLER

JACQUELINE KENNEDY

[Signature of Rachmaninoff]

[Signature of Toscanini]

Musicians:
RACHMANINOFF, left; TOSCANINI, above.

[Signature of Milton Caniff]

MILTON CANIFF,
Cartoonist.

[Signature of Edna St. Vincent Millay]

EDNA ST. VINCENT MILLAY,
Poetess.

[Signature: H·MATISSE]

MATISSE: Artist.

[Signature: Marshall McLuhan]

Author.

[Signature: Picasso]

PICASSO: Artist.

[Signature: George Sand]

Authoress.

[Signature of Beethoven]

BEETHOVEN,
Musician.

["50th anniversary" — Irving Berlin signature]

IRVING BERLIN,
Musician.

[Signature: ammy. / Sammy Cahn]

**SAMMY
CAHN,**
Musician.

[Signature: Percy B. Shelley]

Poet.

[Signature: Albert Schweitzer]

ALBERT SCHWEITZER, Philosopher.

[Japanese characters / Foujita signature]

FOUJITA,
Artist.

[Signature: A. Einstein]

ALBERT EINSTEIN,
Scientist.

[Signature: Annabel Lee / By Edgar A. Poe.]

Author.

[Signature: Serge Prokofieff]

SERGE PROKOFIEFF,
Musician.

[Signature: Oscar Wilde]

Author.

FRANCISCO FRANCO, Dictator.

TARI STEWARD, Artist.

Sports figure.

The Encircled Signature. The circle is a symbol of anxiety, the desire to enclose and shelter the self; it also indicates inner withdrawal from social relationships, which are mistrusted. When the name is fully or particularly crossed out the writer is deflecting his aggressive energies back upon himself in a gesture of self-destruction.

Doctor.

SAM ERVIN, Senator.

ERNEST HEMINGWAY, Writer.

The Direction that the signature takes, ascending or descending, indicates the mood of the writer, optimistic or depressed, and can also be interpreted as health or fatigue level with other signs in the body of the writing.

Sincerely,

Hugh M. Hefner

HUGH M. HEFNER, Publisher.

MARK SPITZ, Athlete.

HENRY FORD II, Industrialist.

Illegible Portions of the name show hostility toward just that part. Diminished units indicate effacement and lack of emphasis placed on that initial or name.

FRANK GIFFORD, Athlete.

DR. GEORGE BACH, Psychologist,
Author of "Creative Aggression"

GEORGE MEANY, Labor leader.

MARK O. HATFIELD, Senator.

The Illegible Signature signifies a desire to be secretive and enigmatic, or, with a poor form level script, inconsideration and egotistical impatience. Some warped forms indicate eccentricity.

EDWARD KENNEDY,
Senator.

HENRY MOORE, Sculptor.

geraldo Rivera

ROBERT KENNEDY, Senator.

X-ing on Letter Forms is a sign of inner fears, disappointments, or depression. In the signature it relates to serious ego-loss such as death of a loved person, defeat, or grave illness and age. X-ing turns up in many suicide notes.

Raphael Soyer   Artist.

CHARLES DE GAULLE,
French leader.

JOSEPH CONRAD, Author.

A Dot Following the Signature reflects an impulse to come to an end, to have the final word and cut off further interaction. It can also indicate distrust and guardedness.

Diahann Carroll

Hubert H Humphrey

George C Wallace

Mary Tyler Moore

Jack Dempsey

Helen Gurley Brown

Dave Brubeck

Audrey Meadows

Ozzie Nelson

Phyllis Diller

Norman Vincent Peale

John F. Kennedy
U.S.S.

Sincerely,
Harry Truman

Jerry Lewis

new york

John Lindsay

Benjamin Spock

Barry Goldwater

Martin Luther King Jr.

John Connolly

Jerry Ford

Conrad N Hilton

Ronald Reagan

Dean Rusk

Pete Seeger

Charles H. Percy

Jimmy Carter

Carol Burnett

Tom Bradley

Cornelia Otis Skinner

Imogene Coca

Madeline Kahn

Helen Reddy

Mamie Eisenhower

Shari Lewis

Gloria Vanderbilt

Red Skelton

Letter Specifics

Just taken by themselves many letters give clues to personality traits. Certain generally accepted letter specifics will be considered in the next pages; an explanation of the meaning of every variation of every letter in the alphabet would require chapters. Also, graphologists show some disagreement themselves as to specific interpretations. The student must test these specifics and add new definitions as they occur.

CAPITALS

Looking at the capitals first, keep in mind that they represent the public side of the writer, the way an individual wishes to appear, as well as revealing unconscious inner attitudes. Capitals are evaluated according to three standards: first, the *size* ... the larger and more inflated they are, the greater the vanity and pride, or, the greater the compensation for inner weakness; second, the *form* ... excessive embellishment indicates affectation, ostentation and a self-consciousness; third, the inherent *originality* and *grace* ... the indicator of the writer's true creativity, artistry, and taste.

In capital letters, as in writing in general, simplification in the letter form shows a mature writer able to see and act on the essentials in life, to be objective, constructive and purposeful. Capitals with added curlicues, flourishes, upward lines, extra loops and hooks show a mind and personality distracted onto various tangents. Sometimes these additions detract from smooth functioning, sometimes they add another dimension to the personality. Capital letters used where they ought not to be are a sign of disordered thinking.

The information below can be applied to all capital letters, not just those illustrated.

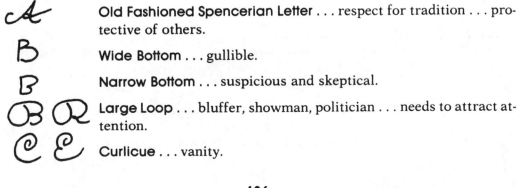

Old Fashioned Spencerian Letter ... respect for tradition ... protective of others.

Wide Bottom ... gullible.

Narrow Bottom ... suspicious and skeptical.

Large Loop ... bluffer, showman, politician ... needs to attract attention.

Curlicue ... vanity.

Open Top . . . generosity and open-heartedness . . . open to new experiences.

Closed Top . . . conservatism and timidity . . . reserved, keeps own counsel.

FJTR   Clear Simple Formation . . . efficiency, good taste, cultural awareness.

K   Long Upper Stroke . . . ambitious.

K   Strokes Do Not Meet . . . problems in social adaption . . . cool and distant.

Swinging Loops . . . charisma and charm . . . ease of body movement.

Wavy Flags . . . good nature and sense of humor.

Second Hump High . . . tenacity and aggressiveness . . . needs to be in control to feel secure.

First Hump High . . . social ambitions . . . lack of tact, poor taste.

Looped . . . absorption with the self . . . vanity.

Wide . . . uninhibited with the body . . . wasteful, boastful.

Narrow with Side Indented . . . self-consciousness, rigidity . . . inhibitions about the body.

TTT   Structural . . . cool efficiency with no frills . . . gets immediately to essentials.

Open Oval . . . talkative.

Palmer Method "S" . . .conventional to the point of dullness.

Long Upper Thrusts . . . ambitious.

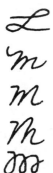 Spikes from Upper Zone . . . importance placed upon intellectual prowess.

Spikes from Lower Zone . . . ties to past and family . . . aggression . . . materialism . . . need for physical security.

U W   Rounded at Baseline . . . poetic . . . sensitive.

THE GRAPHOLOGICAL MEANING OF CERTAIN SMALL LETTERS

The personal pronoun I, the d, the t, the i-dot, and the signature all have special meaning in understanding the self-image of the writer, his social reactions and goals. There are additional character traits that can be learned from the formation of certain other of the small letters. That is to say, over the years as handwriting students continued to test their observations of the psychological meaning of letter formations, certain small letters consistently gave the same evidence.

For example, the letter w came to be associated with the writer's ambition, the letters g and e with culture, the p with athletic inclinations, the square r with manual dexterity, and the letter y in its lower zone particularly, with sexuality. In interpreting these small letter specifics remember that each must appear often as a natural characteristic of the script; do not over-emphasize an occasionally misplaced, self-conscious, or faulty stroke.

Looking at all of the small letters together in a given writing the analyst can make some general observations: evenly sized small letters, all pretty much the same height, show the consistency, sincerity, and conscientiousness of the writer. Overly rigid, machine-like sameness betrays fear and over-control, overly uneven sizing shows moodiness, changeability, and shiftiness.

THREE KINDS OF THINKERS AS SEEN IN THE ROUNDED TOPS OF SMALL m, n, r.

Sharp Needle Points reveal a penetrating, fast, and intuitive thinker, one who sizes up situations and grasps facts instantly. The sharper and higher the points the more vivid and rapid the comprehension.

Upsidedown V, or Spade Shape shows a critical and investigative mind which explores and digs for knowledge, always asking questions and seeking answers; an intellectually thirsty person with eagerness to learn.

Rounded m, n, r's reveal the careful and creative mind that accumulates observations and facts and finally uses each piece logically to build a mental structure. Each piece has to fit. Facts should be proven.

Overly Rounded Tops of the Small m, n, or r show childish tendencies on the part of the writer. There is a lack of mental acuity, immaturity, with the yielding and submissive traits of one who is obedient and follows the rules. Not easily adaptable to circumstances, and can be somewhat dull and lazy.

Sharp Needle Points with Very Rounded Connections indicate an inner conflict between a keen mind and a very yielding nature, between mental maturity and emotional immaturity. The emotional nature cannot carry through with what the mind perceives, and the person feels weak and frustrated.

SMALL LETTER SPECIFICS

Open at Top . . . generosity, frankness, truthfulness and sincerity . . . too wide and rightward: tactlessness . . . talkative.

Tightly Closed . . . caution; with a vertical hand, secretiveness; slyness, craftiness if f and s also knotted.

Open at Bottom . . . dishonesty.

Open Lip . . . credulousness, a tendency to be gullible, trusting . . . without guile . . . lacks sales resistance.

Tightly Closed . . . caution . . . secretiveness.

Loop on C . . . vanity.

Wide Loop on E . . . loves to talk.

Narrow Ink-Filled Letters . . . possibility of violence.

Greek E . . . refinement . . . culture . . . or the aspiration rather than the realization of culture in self-conscious scripts showing desire to be refined . . . one whose ideals are "nice."

F . . . **Letter of Practicality** . . . big upper loop = many theories with little follow-through. Big lower loop = actively practical.

F . . . **Not Looped, Return Stroke to Right** . . . austerity.

Long Down-Strokes . . . looped or straight f, g, p, y: love of outdoor sports . . . practical and down-to-earth personality . . . restless sexuality.

Return Stroke to Left . . . fluency of thought . . . quick mind.

Figure 9 "G" . . . mathematical ability . . . people who tend to be highly critical and see everything in black and white . . . good judgment.

Figure 8 "G" . . . ability to adapt, rapidity of thought, literary tastes, intellectual flexibility, fine intuition and instinct, innate understanding and gentleness . . . philosophy and sense of humor.

G Made Like Q or Q Made Like G . . . peculiar or contrary value structure . . . a confusion in the basic drives . . . can mean a messianic or martyr complex.

Return Stroke Retraces . . . the impulse is to give but caution rules against it . . . retracing = hiding and inhibition.

Squared-off Lower Loop . . . aggressiveness and obstinacy plus a measure of compulsiveness . . . does not give up . . . judgmental.

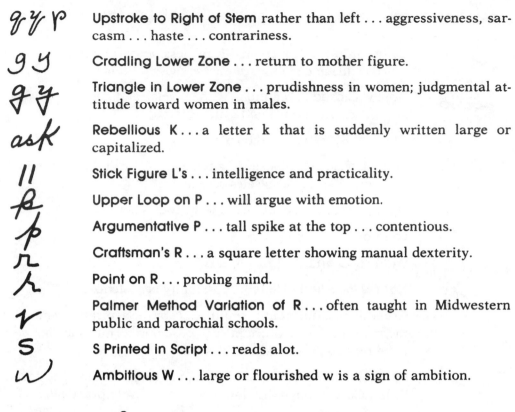

Upstroke to Right of Stem rather than left . . . aggressiveness, sarcasm . . . haste . . . contrariness.

Cradling Lower Zone . . . return to mother figure.

Triangle in Lower Zone . . . prudishness in women; judgmental attitude toward women in males.

Rebellious K . . . a letter k that is suddenly written large or capitalized.

Stick Figure L's . . . intelligence and practicality.

Upper Loop on P . . . will argue with emotion.

Argumentative P . . . tall spike at the top . . . contentious.

Craftsman's R . . . a square letter showing manual dexterity.

Point on R . . . probing mind.

Palmer Method Variation of R . . . often taught in Midwestern public and parochial schools.

S Printed in Script . . . reads alot.

Ambitious W . . . large or flourished w is a sign of ambition.

THE SEXUAL ASPECTS OF y

Everyone unconsciously gives away information about his sexual personality by the way he writes. Sharp, unkind angles, domineering t-bars, letters jammed together seeking closeness, or fearful, spaced-out printing are all clues to the writer's attitude toward physical intimacy. As simple a feature as how the person emphasizes or neglects words of sentiment like "dear" and "love" and personal names shows the quality of his emotional/sexual involvement. Also, look for the strength of the sexual drive in the degree of pressure and pastiosity in the writing.

The LZ has been established as the area in which biological urges and instinctual drives are expressed. Here there are three broad clues to sexual behavior: the length and formation of LZ loops, particularly on the letter y and g, the slant of these loops and the pressure exerted by the pen.

The length of the LZ formations gives a measure of the strength and potential of the sexual drive, the formation of the loop expresses the degree of sexual satisfaction. If the lower loop is fully rounded and returns to the baseline it indicates an active and healthy sex life. Hugely inflated, heavily written LZ loops show a forceful sex drive and a vivid sexual imagination. Short, lightly-pressured LZ formations are evidence of the sublimation of sexual energies into ideas, projects, the daily life and work. When the return stroke of the loop does not reach the baseline but crosses below, sexual fulfillment is lacking.

LZ loops that pull leftward reveal a sexual dependency upon the partner for initiation of the sexual act and for continued encouragement, support and approval. Stems or loops drawing toward the right margin show a suppression of erotic drives in favor of social or ideal concerns. Long, embellished and elaborated loops reveal self-consciousness about sex; the more bizarre these appear to be the more eccentric and ornamented the sexual fantasy. Marked irregularity of forms shows sexual excitability and confusion, whereas monotonous regularity in the size and shape of loops points to dullness in response or over-control.

The MZ head of the y and g discloses how successfully the LZ sexual energy has found an object in everyday life. Well-formed upper portions of these letters carry the drives to realistic, active expression. Flattened, threaded, or barely-existing MZ anchors for the LZ loops reveal an unsettled focus, the lack of an outlet for the drives, or, with large loops, more fantasy than reality.

The small letter y is a key to much specific information about the writer's sexual interests, habits, and abilities. The small letter g, which also has many lower zone possibilities, is an aid as well; but is primarily a cultural letter. Remember that any middle zone letters or parts that are pulled or distorted into the lower zone will add an emphasis to the lower zone/sexual preoccupation of the writing.

While examining the y for sexual information remember that the lower zone also gives information about attitudes toward money and possessions (materialism) and security (feelings of personal worth and belonging) and is a source of energy and creativity. The following letter specifics, however, will concentrate upon the sexual interpretation of the letter y.

Normal Palmer Method LZ . . . a warm and receptive nature free of fear and inhibition . . . flexible.

Long Heavy Plunge into LZ . . . determination, firmness and aggressiveness . . . sometimes defensiveness.

Unfinished LZ Loop . . . unrealistic, possibly wishful, sexual expectations that are unfulfilled.

Downward Ending . . . discouragement, depression, or anger toward current sexual partner.

my y — **X-ing** . . . a grave disappointment in past sexual life or deep fears. (Lower body illness or alcohol problems.)

my y — **Tic Leftward or Rightward** . . . sexual frustration, temper and impatience.

my y — **No Middle Zone Formation** . . . no focus for sexual energy or fantasy in the daily life . . . deprived.

my y — **Lower Zone Ends Light** . . . sexual energy starts strong but dissipates quickly . . . need for continual change of sexual partner.

my y — **Lower Zone Ends Long and Light** . . . extreme sexual restlessness, vulnerable to strong drives of others . . . when curved = poetic and open to instinctual expression as well.

loving you — **Small Closed Loop** . . . lack of sexual fulfillment . . . large loops tied off means materialism (money bags).

my y — **Retracing in Lower Zone** . . . severe repression of unconscious sexual and emotional needs . . . unlikely to enjoy sex due to overcontrol and fear.

loving you — **Normal Smooth Loops** . . . sexually active, fulfilled, can divert energy . . . very long = restless.

loving you — **Long Full Round Heavy Loops** . . . gets emotionally involved . . . sexuality dominates . . . energy released physically.

loving you excelling — **Tangled Large Loops** . . . sexuality off-balance . . . disturbed . . . possibly sexual obsessions.

loving you — **Left Curve** . . . leans to past . . . dependency on others for sexual strength.

loving you — **Lower Zone Short: Often Without Loop** . . . sublimation of sex or a tendency to suppress sexual drives . . . practicality and daily life involvement.

my girl Jill — **Jerky, Tremulous, Broken Loops with Light Pressure** . . . weakness in drives . . . disturbed coordination (physical illness or anxiety).

g y g g — **Vagaries in Lower Zone** . . . when consistent, show sexual fantasy . . . can be perversion.

really, variety is great.. — **Variety in Lower Zone** . . . normal forms = heterosexual versatility and adaptability . . . degree reveals writer's susceptibility to stimulation and readiness for response . . . marked irregularity = excitability and lack of control.

my loving you — **Monotonous Regularity in Loop Size** . . . married into habit pattern . . . dull temperament . . . over-control . . . sexually conventional.

loving you   **Cradle** . . . unresolved emotional tie with mother figure . . . men cannot freely give sexual feeling to another woman; women look for mother replacement.

my girl Jill   **Heavy Down Stroke with Light Return** . . . strong drive with little follow through . . . with tiny loop shows disfunction.

my girl Mary   **Angles in Lower Zone; Strokes End Left** . . . withdrawal . . . anger . . . *Felon's Claw:* unconscious guilt and sexual aberration.

loving you   **Triangle in Lower Zone** . . . anger and unresolved sexual anxiety . . . men have double standard regarding women; they want Virgin Mary as a wife, and speak loosely of women, yet they are sexually attracted to "bad" women. Women with this writing characteristic are prudish and rejective.

you're going   **Lower Zone Ends Right** . . . drawing away from sex . . . sexually repressed and evasive . . . energy moves quickly back to middle zone . . . sublimation of drives toward social concerns and altruism . . . (with rightward flags and disconnected d: homosexuality).

Danger Signs

HONESTY AND DISHONESTY

The Honest Person is legitimate, truthful, fair, and straightforward in his conduct. He behaves with integrity, avoids subterfuge, duplicity, fraud or deception. Honest writing is clear and legible. There is uniformity of style—especially within the middle zone. Baselines are even and pressure is firm and steady. There is an absence of flourishes or ornamentation. Slant is consistent as are size and spacing.

This is just to see if my writing has changed much in

The Dishonest Person has a disposition to defraud, deceive, betray, forge, lie, embezzle, steal, or be faithless. The person who is aware of his deceitful inclinations reveals symptoms of emotional upset or nervous tension. These symptoms express through the writing as erratic changes in slant, pressure, sizing, and spatial relationships. Sometimes the person represses his dishonest intentions and compensates with control as revealed by signs of rigidity in these four basic areas.

I think you misunderstood my intentions and I think that I really do want everything to work out between us. You must know that you are very important to

Some personality traits that contribute to dishonesty are:

Vanity - large writing with inflated loops, flourishes, circle i-dots.

Acquisitiveness or Materialism - prolonged endings, coiled ovals, hooks, long lower zone, closed forms, tangling.

Weak Will Power - erratic and often dished t-bars, sinuous baseline, erratic sizing, threading.

Emotional Instability - tangling, erratic letter spacing, t-bar vacillation, rhythmic disturbance, excessive looping, erratic spacing, extreme changes in pressure pattern, erratic slant.

Shrewdness - coiled ovals, excessive angularity, threading.

Secretive Nature - coiled ovals, closed forms, tight writing, arcading, threading.

Resentment - angularity, temper tics, sudden pressure.

Anti-social Attitudes - angularity, rhythmic disturbance, counter strokes, large and loopy middle zone that often connects with angularity.

DETERMINING HONESTY AND DISHONESTY

There are many signs in writing which can indicate dishonesty in addition to extreme fluctuation or rigidity in the four basic areas of slant, size, pressure and spacing. It is necessary to see an accumulation of many of these signs in order to determine dishonesty. The more signs present, the stronger the dishonest tendencies within the writer.

Dishonesty Can Be Suspected in Writing that is:

Indistinct or Illegible - noncommittal nature, inability or unwillingness to communicate in a straightforward fashion.

Too Slow, Neat or Artificial - pretentious, calculated to deceive, plays a double role in a jekyll-and-hyde personality, hesitancy, lack of spontaneity, desire to create illusion.

Too Complex or Too Simplified in Letter Shapes to the extent that they become ambiguous - deception.

Sinuous Baselines or Highly Erratic Baselines - opportunism, follows lines of least resistance, finds excuses, too adaptable and unstable in terms of moral and mood strengths.

Rigid Baselines - premeditation, calculation, forces self into socially acceptable behavior not naturally felt: a denial, usually covering up an undesirable impulse person doesn't want to be blamed for.

(A Reminder: The normal, flexible baseline is a sign of moral adjustment and consistency of mood level.)

Uneven Pressure - falls too easily under the influence of others: weak sense of will power and short-lived goals: person gives up too easily, or vacillates under pressure of inner drives.

Muddy Pressure - desire to satisfy strong urges, often seen in slurred letters or ink-filled ovals.

Very Light Pressure - falls too easily under the influence of others.

Threaded Strokes or Letters Within Words with Clear Initial and Endings Letters - presents a clear outer facade yet is devious within: ambiguous motives, imprecise.

Combination of Extreme Angularity with Extreme Arcades - aggression and resentment, hypocrisy: a sign of criminality or mental disturbance.

Many or Extreme Arcades - artificiality, hiding something.

Flattened Arcades that Look like Garlands - secretive, underhanded.

Over-Garlanded - extra defensive due to guilt feelings, will sometimes lie to keep from being blamed.

(A Reminder: Healthiest combination is a variety of garlands, arcades and angles with threading only sometimes near the ends of words and with all formations being smooth and direct.)

Cramped Letters or Cramped Connections - pettiness and narrowmindedness that fears discovery.

Wide Spaces between Words and Lines - personal detachment.

Cramped or Tangled Spacing - complexity of action.

Coiling, Complicated Forms - trickiness or cunning.

Counterstrokes (Reversals from the Normal Direction) - anti-social nature, rebellious to authority, misdirected energies.

Upward or Downward Cover Strokes (Retracing) - something to conceal, expression is inhibited.

Weak or Absent T-bars - weak or vacillating will-power or goals.

Misplaced Periods (especially inside letters) - compulsion, calculation, guilt.

Awkward or Often Omitted Small Letters or Pieces of Letters Omitted - person leaves out essential parts of information, ability to slide past commitment.

Uneven Letter Sizing with some Threading - manipulative.

Slurred or Ink-filled Letters - habitual concealing.

Many Letters Corrected or Retouched (except in cases to provide more legibility) - intention to cover-up.

Ovals Excessively Looped, Stabbed, Upside Down, or backwards - all signs of a secretive, concealing nature.

Extreme Difference between Signature and Script - person not the same in public life as in private life, discrepancy between presentation of self and actual self.

Broken or Fragmented Letters (especially at the base or to the left) - a sign of anxiety and lack of certainty.

Prolonged Left-tending Final Strokes (especially in capitals) - acts on aggression which stems from feelings about the family or the past. (The felon's claw is a very good example of this.)

Initial Strokes which Start Strangely (such as lead-ins from below the baseline or strokes that begin leftward before going rightward) - reluctance to proceed normally.

Reclined Writing - confusion over role in life, unwillingness to show true feelings.

Dominating Upper or Lower Zone (or both) to the Detriment of the Middle - ideals and desires are not in line with fulfillment in reality.

Long, Full Lower Zones that are often Angular - frustrated materialism, anger.

Over-inflated Upper Loops - delusional thinking not in line with reality.

Do not forget that in order to determine actual dishonesty and not just emotional instability, tension or anxiety, you must see an accumulation of many of the above signs.

Liars and Lying

Lying - the habitual liar is a social type. He is unwilling to communicate frankly and shows this with indirect and hesitant conversation. In writing, the liar doesn't take a direct route either.

When a Person Leaves Out Essential Parts in Relating Something - the first letter is deceptively clear but later letters are indistinct or omitted.

When One Essential Part is Left Out and an Invented One is Substituted - some letters are replaced with ones that don't belong there.

When an Essential is Left Out and the Gap is Filled with Chit-Chat - a letter (or more) is left out and instead there is a thread.

Pathological liars are compensating for feelings of inferiority. Look for signs of extreme ambition:

> **Tall Capitals** - wants to be very important or even famous.
> **High T-bars** often left of the stem - high aspirations not followed through.
> **Very Tall Upper Zone** - imagination and ambition, high ideals for self.
> **Very Looped Upper Zone** - fantasy and illusion rule thinking.
> **Erratic or Very Flattened Middle Zone** - dissatisfaction with daily life.
> **T-bars Often Above the Stem** - unrealistic goals.
> **Greatly Reduced Pressure on Upstrokes and Rightward Strokes** - can't follow through.
> **Very Slow Writing** - calculated for appearance, premeditation.
> **Too Much Roundness** - immaturity, lack of ego strength.
> **Rhythmic Disturbance** (too dispersed and uncontrolled or too rigid) - anxiety, tension.

The pathological liar identifies with the roles he assumes and will often show:

> **Two Different Styles of Writing (or more)** - more than one personality.
> **A Very Flamboyant Signature** - theatrical public self.
> **Erratic Changes in Pressure** (with more tendency to lighten up on the stroke) - sudden changes in intensity and mode of expression.
> **Tall Upper Zone with Short Lower Zone** - identifies with illusions, not rooted in reality, impractical.

Large, Embellished, Bizarre, Inflated or Highly Ornamented Writing - indicates delusions of grandeur.

Extreme Arcading - hypocrisy.

Very Light Pressure - ability to change way of feeling and expressing without much effort.

SAMPLES SHOWING DISHONESTY

A woman who is selfish, materialistic, doesn't return things, exaggerates and fibs.

A man who is sneaky, clever, and suspicious. He wiggles out of responsibility by blaming others.

A young man with a history of shoplifting.

I'll bring your book by soon —
I take you up on that cup of
coffee.
Thank you both for
being your

Writing of a counsellor who is attracted to young girls in violation of his moral responsibilities.

Not that the human experience
has not taught us, but our
ability to recognize the counsellor
is are negligible.

A man who is dishonest in his personal and business life.

Greed - shown by inflated numbers, inflated lower zone, hooks on lead-in or ending strokes, leftward-tending strokes, large writing with few ending strokes, inflated loops, coiling, tangling.

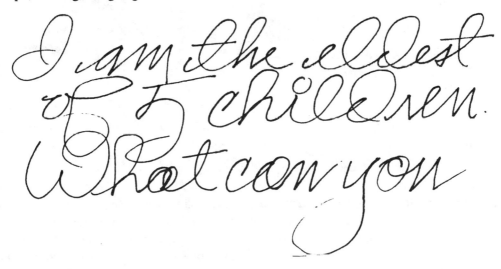

I am the eldest
of 5 children.
What can you

Forgers - Signs which make it possible for one to forge the writing of another:

Smooth Rhythm - possesses motor coordination necessary to control writing movement.

Angular Letter Formations - mechanical skill, attention to detail, perfectionistic and observant nature.

Tapering Words - quick thinker, directness of action.

Natural Shading - artistic, creative, imitative ability.

Exaggerated and Sweeping Capitals - coordination, love of body movement.

Yes it would be possible for me to forge some-one elses writing if I wanted to, but I don't

Naturally, not all people with these qualities in their writing will be forgers, but if they were so inclined, it would be possible for them to imitate the writing of another. In order to determine whether it's in their nature to forge, check the list of 34 dishonest signs and locate at least 8 of them in the suspect writing.

SIGNS OF VIOLENCE

Major Signs:

Highly Pastiose Writing which looks Muddy and Smeary - indulgence of sensuality and libido urges.

sensually indulgent

Heavy Pressure that is often Variable or Misplaced - intense feelings with strong reactions. These writers seek to make their mark on life around them. When the pressure is displaced from the downstrokes (contracting strokes) to the upstrokes or horizontal strokes (release strokes) we see that expressive force is directed against the environment. Variable or erratic pressure indicates fluctuation in the ability to express feelings and in the intensity of expression.

variable and misplaced on ups or release strokes

Remember that it is natural to be lighter on the upstroke and heavier on the downstroke—lighter on the release stroke and heavier on the contracting stroke.

Also Look For:

Heavy Descending T-bars - domineering nature, aggressive force.

that bat

Clubbing in Lower Zone Endings - aggression released physically.

getting chubby

Clubbing in T-bars - force of will is hostile and aggressive.

what a fat cat

Downward Endings - stubborn, temperamental, sarcastic.

Don't make me mad

Downward, Thick, and Clubbed Endings - brutality, tenacity, sadism, too much energy left over at the end, violence, cruelty.

feeling cruel today

Sharp Endings Descending Vertically - intolerance, strong likes and dislikes, bad temper.

you're never right, I am!

Long, Sharp Stick-Figure Strokes into the Lower Zone (dagger-like appearance) - disturbance in libido takes a sarcastic, slashing form of expression.

you have many penny   or any

Slashing Strokes and Pressure Horizontally - energy directed against the environment.

more anger than I'd felt

Generally Heavy Pressure - when seen with other signs of violence, heavy pressure indicates that the writer has the force and inclination to demonstrate the anger he feels inside.

When I'm angry -watch out !

Extremely Long Lower Zone that Doesn't Complete with a Loop - strong libidinal urges that have bottled up due to inability to express them normally in daily life.

going in any way on a grey day.

The Maniacal "d" or Other Maniacal Letters (these letters slant more to the right than the rest of the writing) - capable of sudden changes in temperament which result in impulsive and erratic behavior. Because the "d" is a social self-image letter, it is more serious when the sudden move to the right occurs on this letter.

One day when I'd had it!

Clubbed "d" which Stands on its Own Stem - obstinancy and desire to control situations combined with a calculated, cruel nature.

I'd been bad or had I?

Letters or Words which have been Gone Over more than Once - an indication the writer has experienced a lapse of consciousness. When seen in combination with other signs of violence such as extreme pastiosity or misplaced pressure within a generally heavy pattern, the writer can become very dangerous and may not remember later what happened. The mental processes are not smooth, and the thinking is obsessional. The instincts are ready to express without the usual restraint of will-power.

was my shepherd - not there.

Misplaced Capital Letters within Words - violent nature, sudden and impulsive outbursts, over-reactive.

A lATE date wAS my faTE.

When misplaced capitals occur at the beginnings of words it is not nearly as serious. Still, this person places too much importance upon his own actions and overreacts emotionally.

I've Been Feeling a great Deal

Extreme Changes in the Sizes of Middle Zone Letters - socially erratic behavior, anti-social tendencies.

I don't like to follow rules.

Tiny, Ink-filled Ovals with some Large Ovals - tension, excitability, verbally explosive.

you're just too much, you know

Extreme Angularity - aggression. When found with heavy pressure, pastiosity, and other signs of temper or violence, the aggression is expressed physically.

I was here, you were there.
I WAS HERE, YOU WERE THERE.

Rhythmic Disturbance with More Angles and Arcades than Usual (if garlands are present, they are usually flattened-out or squared-off) - tension within the writer, potentially explosive situation due to pent-up emotions and anxiety: frustration, feelings of isolation (seen in angles at the tops of upper zone loops and the bottoms of lower zones): extreme angularity with extreme arcades = emotional disturbance.

More angles and arcades than usual and pointed loops .

Minor Signs: (Any of these need to be supported with major signs)

Reclined Personal Pronoun "I" with Over-Sensitive "d" - repression over self-image with too much sensitivity and pride, ego still too attached to the mother figure: with other signs, explosive outbursts.

I Don't like bad Indians

Inattention to Margins which are Often Crowded or Otherwise Peculiar Looking - disdain for authority and rules.

Sudden Changes from Writing to Printing - divided nature, not sure whether to be socially expressive or socially withdrawn.

well, when you say that I'm not sure what you mean or if you really feel that way

Printed Writing with No Connections - hides personality, fear of exposure and involvement, secretive and guarded.

I started printing when I was
I STARTED PRINTING WHEN I WAS

Defiant k - rebellious to authority figures and traditional values.

take a husky drink.

Argumentative p - will engage in verbal combat.

my appetite is petite, but my phight is a plight.

The Shark's Tooth - biting trait to the character (a combination of a cover-stroke and an angle).

cccchicces drink evil.

Bizarre Letters - distortions in thinking.

That Great Lag WAS Just
AND THEN THE BAD WERE

False Embellishment - egocentrism, hiding, tension released on non-essentials: con artists often embellish.

Consider this if you will

Lines Coming Too Close to the Right Edge - impulsive, has a hard time holding back.

Once I get started it's hard

Presence of Check-mark or X-like Formations - thoughts of endings or death, depression.

I was here at last, ready to

Kathy, Clarence & I if we were any of use had be Contacted I said no, Kathy said NO, but Clarence stated that he had found a note on his door over the weekend from Harry to call him Emergency. Clarence stated that he called the number on the note & Harry

A man who is anti-social and explosive.

FRANKLIN
ROOSEVELT,
American President.

inclined to think after it is at present be insider change my Kick House in touch Monday.

Roosevelt

The cold winds of War are blowing; It is the time to draw forth the broken Shields and March forth to the Rising *The Battle surrounds me, Shield at my back; .... Though at Ebb and my fire frozen true as long as there is my Idea all Men. _____*

Writing of a man with a violent temper. He gets carried away emotionally, blows up about it, and then apologizes later. He has frequent temper outbursts and verbal rages. He's jealous and possessive, ardent and romantic. He's secretive at first and then very open.

EMOTIONAL INSTABILITY

Three behavior characteristics are commonly considered in defining emotional instability: distress of the person himself, disturbance of others due to his own distress, and the resultant handicaps experienced by the person in trying to organize and experience his own life.

It makes sense to view emotional instability as a continuum in which incapacitation and distress are extreme at one end and minimal at the other. Most of us fall in the middle with some mild inhibitions or anxieties that do not seriously handicap us.

The biggest clue to emotional instability as revealed by writing is rhythmic disturbance. If you determine a problem in the rhythm, it is still necessary to support this with several other signs of instability. The more signs you are able to find within one sample, the more extreme are the indications of emotional problems.

Most of the following signs have already been discussed to some extent in each of their separate areas. Here they are listed together to help you determine the extent of disturbance to the emotional balance of an individual.

SIGNS OF EMOTIONAL INSTABILITY

Rhythm - Rhythm has been described as a balance between the contracting and releasing qualities of the writing. In the following extremes of rhythmic disturbance, the person is out of harmony with himself and with his surroundings.

Extreme Release indicates absence of control and strong feelings of anxiety. The person is experiencing a strong or dominating blend of uncertainty, agitation, dread, and a brooding fear about some contingency. His behavior is uneasy, unrealistic, and irrational.

I m. Very Happy
I want to wish
Happy Birthday hope

Extreme Contraction indicates absence of spontaneity and strong feelings of tension. Here the person is experiencing increased psychological stress and inner unrest. Extra control is placed on the actions due to a fear of expressing the hostility being felt.

I am a
housewife
I live in
a house.

In addition to rhythmic disintegration and rhythmic rigidity, other qualities of rhythmic disturbance are:

Splinting of Letters - fractured mental processes.

Retouching - uncertainty, lack of confidence, nervousness, anxiety.

Tremor - tremor is a muscular agitation brought on by mental or physical problems. It indicates fatigue, dependency, weakness and passivity.

Zonal Imbalance - lack of harmony in three basic areas of ego development.
Inflated Upper Zone - delusional thinking dominated by fantasy and illusion, lack of secure hold on reality.

Inflated Middle Zone - lack of maturity.
Inflated Lower Zone - insecurity, instinctual drives out of control.
Shrunken Upper Zone - lacks inspiration, no confidence in mental abilities.
Shrunken Middle Zone - inability to cope with daily life, unhappiness.
Shrunken Lower Zone - sexual immaturity, fear, trauma.

Highly Erratic Baselines - lack of moral adjustment, inconsistent attitudes.
Very Rigid Baselines - narrow-mindedness, tension, inhibition, fears.
Extreme Rising of Baselines - flightiness, restlessness, lack of firm hold on reality.
Falling Baselines - depression, unhappiness.

Erratic Slant - nervous, unsettled, erratic mode of expression.
Extremely Inclined Slant (more than 45 degrees over from the vertical) - reactive, hysterical, impulsive, unsettled, fanatical, obsessive.
Extremely Reclined Slant (more than 35 degrees back from the vertical) - withdrawn, evasive, emotional development is blocked.

Extremely Heavy Pressure - internally inhibited, potentially explosive.
Sudden Bursts of Pressure within a Heavy Pattern - paranoid personality.
Extremely Light Pressure - erratic feeling response.
Highly Irregular Pressure - evasive behavior, lack of involvement.
Pressure Misplaced Into Horizontal Dimension - anxiety, hysteria, possible schizoid personality disorder.
Pressure so Light it Breaks in Places - anxiety, nervousness, doubts over own ability to face difficulty.
Extreme Pastiosity - highly sensual nature, possible violence, sexual perversion, alcohol or drug abuse, criminality, mental or physical illness.

Crowded or Tangled Writing - confusion, lack of inner harmony and balance.
Uneven Margins - anti-social behavior, rebelliousness.
No Margins or Space Anywhere - fears, especially of death, overly talkative.
Gigantic Writing - mania, lack of awareness of boundaries between self and the environment, exhibitionism.
Microscopic Writing - introversion, fear, inhibition, creation of private world, lack of ability to relate realistically to others.
Extreme Variation of Letter Size - inconsistent in responses to environment, oversensitive, indecisive, childish, moody.
Narrow Letters - self-critical, up-tight, self-conscious, repressed.
Too Much Space Everywhere - fear of enclosure, isolation, withdrawal, suspicion.
Erratic Spacing - lack of inner organization, inner conflict, moodiness.
Rigid Spacing and Placement on Page - fears losing control of self or surroundings.
Illegible Writing - out of touch with reality, inability to communicate needs and ideas.

Overly Round Writing - immaturity, dependency, lack of intellectual development, compulsive tendencies, naivete.

Drooping Garlands - feels guilty, lets self be taken advantage of.

Prominent Arcades - exhibitionism, avoidance of dealing with emotional problems, hides behind a facade.

Exaggerated Loops - emotional needs not being satisfied.

Stunted Loops - ability to express emotion is impaired.

Retraced Loops - inhibition, fears emotional involvement.

Distortions in loops - warped emotional response; neurosis.

Reversed Loops - rebelliousness, anti-social tendencies.

Broken Loops - anxiety over a future course of action.

Knotted Ovals - defensive and inhibited.

Small Ink-Filled Ovals - explosive temperament.

Extreme Angularity - out of touch with emotions and feelings of love, aggressive, critical.

Extreme Squaring of Letters and Connecting Strokes - possible psychosis.

Frequent X-ing - self-destructive tendencies, feelings of martyrdom.

Extreme Threading - lack of direction or purpose, lack of hold on reality.

Inconsistent Threading - anxiety, hysteria.

Long Lead-in Strokes - strong dependency ties, exhibitionism.

Lead-in Stroke From Below Baseline - repressed aggression with tension and anxiety: needs to establish healthier relationships with men.

No Ending Strokes - inability to give of oneself to others.

Exaggerated Endings - defensive behavior, fear of being hurt.

Weak Endings - passivity, fear of life, depression.

Heavy or Angular Endings - aggression, hostility directed to environment.

Lower Zone Loops Which Don't Return to the Baseline, or Don't Cross the Stem - frustration of basic drives, thwarted physical energy.

Lower Zones That Turn Away From the Baseline - sexual hostility and resentment.

Horizontal Slashes and Dashes - emotional ability and excitability.

Exaggerated Leftward Movement - fear of the future, defensive, hang-ups on the past.

Many Hooks - tenacity, fear of change, craves security.

Predominantly Angular Connecting Strokes - social aggression, argumentative, out of touch with feelings of self and others.

Arcades With Angles - lack of clear understanding of emotion.

Extremely Connected Writing - compulsive tendencies, too much focus on objectives and too little on the actual situation at hand, delayed emotional reactions.

Totally Disconnected Writing - difficulty in linking experiences meaningfully, introversion, isolation, withdrawal.

Printing - lack of social adjustment, introversion.

Sporadic Alternation Between Printing and Writing - confusion over social roles, inconsistency in thinking.

Reclined "I" - neurosis, personal disharmony and conflict, lack of insight into own problems.

Reversal in Direction of "I" (makes bottom part first) - covert defiance.

Exaggerated Upper Part of "I" - continues to be influenced by father-figures.

Exaggerated Lower Part of "I" - continues to be influenced by mother-figures.

Elaborated or Over-Embellished "I" - uncertain self-image, needs a lot of attention.

Distortion of "I" - distorted self-image, struggling with self-image.

Enlarged Loop on "d" - great pride, overly-sensitive social self-image.

Stem Made First Then Oval Part on "d" (felon's claw formation) - self-punishing, challenging and provoking personality, deviant behavior.

Oval of "d" Enclosed in Big Looped Stem - neurotic social fears, anti-social impulses.

Maniac "d" - sudden emotional outbursts, volatile nature.

Cracked Stem on "d" - lack of social adjustment, neurotic.

Long Strokes Through the Signature - unhappiness with self-image or self-destructive tendencies.

Signature Which is Very Different From Script - unrealistic self-image.

Mixture of T-Bars - lack of consistency of will.

Short T-Bars - restraint of instinct, lack of confidence.

Weak Pressure on T-Bar - resignation, weak will power.

Descending with Light Pressure on T-Bar - hopeless resignation, fear, dependency.

T-Bar Left of Stem - procrastination, indecision.

No T-Bar Crossing - absent-mindedness, despondency, rebellion.

Dished T-Bar - lack of resistance, guilt, instability.

Wild T-Bars - emotional disturbance, lack of direction.

Variety of Letter Style or Formation - lack of continuity in thinking, restlessness.

Remember that in order to determine emotional instability it is necessary to first observe rhythmic disturbance. In addition, there must be many other signs of personality instability seen within the rhythmically disturbed sample. The more signs you are able to find which indicate instability the more disturbed is the emotional nature.

RICHARD NIXON, American President:
changes in signature, from top:
1968, 1969, early 1974, late 1974.

JOSEF STALIN, Russian leader.

LUDWIG II, the "Mad"
King of Bavaria,
four signatures at
various ages.

*Singe mir ein neues Lied: die Welt ist verklärt
und alle Himmel freuen sich.*

NIETZSCHE, German
philosopher and poet.
Above: 1889, shortly
before mental collapse.
Left: 1891 after going mad.

FIDEL CASTRO,
Cuban leader.

soothing soft strong that's right now

—GARY,

LOVE UTTERLY

YOU, —NICOLE, my ELF!

FOREVER, TILL IT IS ALL AS IT
SHOULD AND WILL BE ULTIMATEL
THEN IT WILL ONLY BE BEGINN!!

YOUR ↄ —GAF

I promise you —
there is a place of
no darkness ~

GARY GILMORE,
"Right to die
killer."

Oh ~ Nicole — I addressed the
envelope ~Nicole Gilmore I want you
to use my name I want you to have
my name okay? I give it to you.
~Nicole Gilmore ~ NICOLE GILMORE
~Nicole Gilmore. MRS. GARY GILMORE

STEVE GROGAN, Manson
Gang member.

I love myself very
much please love
me too.

Steve Grogan

LYNETTE "SQUEAKY" FROMME,
Attempted assassin and
Manson Gang member.

Knows the bad. I never called my friend Christ. But
I ask this — where did Jesus Christ pass before leaving us
last? Barrabas was with Public Opinion in the money.
Lynette Fromme

FoR hEAVEMS

SAKe cateh Me

BeFoRe I Kill MoRe

I cannot control myself

RICHARD SPECK,
Mass murderer.

disposed of properly

Robert Fitzgerald.

Kennedy must soon die

die die die die

die die die die die

I Lee Harvey Oswald do hereby request that my present citizenship in the United States of America, be revoked.

I have entered the Soviet Union for the express purpose of applying for citizenship in the Soviet Union, through the means of naturalization

I affirm that my allegiance is to the Union of Soviet Socialist Republics.

LEE HARVEY OSWALD,
Alleged assassin of
President John Kennedy.

No one but a few people like you would dare choose to believe that one like Sam exists.

People do not want to believe of his presence on earth.

So what am I to do?

Do you recall when Mr. Santucci read to the public the psychiatrists a report saying that I felt "emotionally dead"?

Really, it is only the feeling of hopelessness that I possess because of my inability to successfully warn the world.

Sincerely
D.B.

DAVID BERKOWITZ,
Convicted killer.

SON OF SAM

MY CAPTURE I PROMISE
ALL THE GUYS WORKING
HE CASE A NEW PAIR OF
S IF I CAN GET UP THE

DAVID BERKOWITZ
as his "Son of Sam"
murderer personality.

Children's Handwriting

INFANT TO THIRD GRADE

Most of the same rules applied to analyzing adult writing are used for children's writing, but with allowance made, of course, for the roundness, irregularity and unsteadiness of stroke natural to the youngster's untrained motor control. Starting in first grade, American children are usually taught the Palmer method, which is modeled by the teacher on the blackboard as well. The initial printed characters give way to a cursive hand as the child's speed and skill increase.

Even pre-school scribbles reveal the child's in-born temperament and disposition. The active, vigorous tot seizes his crayon and attacks the paper with gusto, covering it with swirls and slashes; the passive, sensitive child exerts slighter effort, content to fill a small portion of the sheet with delicate marks. Both extremes express normal temperament and activity needs.

Early scribbles and drawings, like adult doodles, can be analyzed in terms of movement, forms, and arrangement on the page. The cheerful scribbler covers his paper with wide springy curves, the anxious scribbler constricts his pattern, the sad child reduces the size of his picture and gives the lines a downhill cast, and the angry one increases the angularity and vehemence of his strokes.

Once in first grade and learning to write, a child continues to draw each letter as a separate picture, but with lines to keep him in the proper place on the paper. At the age of six the average child has motor development and eye-hand control that are mature enough to make both up and down strokes; prior to six the strokes upward are hard to manage.

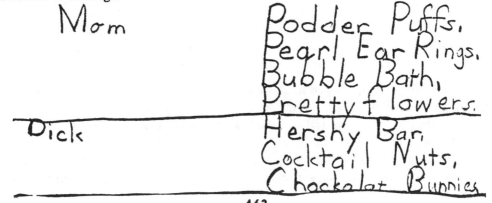

In third grade, at the age of eight, when the alphabet is familiar and natural coordination and control have matured further, individual personality, intelligence, and thinking patterns will start to distinguish the writing. The printed form continues to be practiced because the sideways movement of connecting strokes is still developing. The eight year old below shows normal development, clarity and organization for her age.

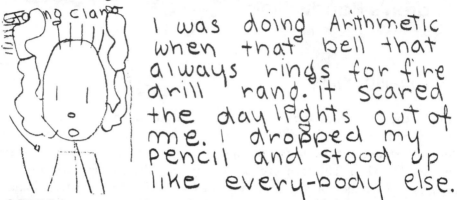

I was doing Arithmetic when that bell that always rings for fire drill rang. It scared the daylights out of me. I dropped my pencil and stood up like every-body else.

FIFTH GRADE

The average nine year old in fourth grade has mastered both upstrokes and turns; he knows the alphabet and can read. He has ceased drawing letter formations as separate little units, for now his eye and hand are well-enough coordinated with the idea in his mind that he can express himself in entire words and sentences.

By the age of ten or eleven round curves dominate and there is a developed pressure pattern. More often than not, the original copybook pattern no longer feels right to the child so he has unconsciously begun to make letters his own way, altering speed, shapes and pressure to fit his personal needs. The child who carries the conventional Palmer method all through his school years, and many times through his adult life, is likely to be quite satisfied with his routine surroundings and tasks and feels no incentive to be different. Also, many times these conventional writers remember how they were praised for their "beautiful hand" by teachers and parents, and so have maintained it with pleasure.

Usually there is a gradual change and gathering of individuality until, by the age of ten, the writing is unique. Personality differences, varying levels of maturity and perception, concentration, and motor control are best revealed when studied comparatively. The following samples were written by a fifth grade class of ten year olds, to a classmate sick in bed at home. The students used pen and ink and strove for good form as this was a penmanship lesson.

This first sample was chosen to show a mature ten year old girl. The consistent, clearly-shaped letters indicate a smart and logical mind and a good self-image; she has dropped the curlicues and frills of the Palmer method and is a practical and efficient young lady. The pressure pattern is normal; the writing is neither too relaxed nor too rigid. The points on the m's and n's indicate a quick mind. The rightward slant and close spacing between sentences show her need to be in touch emotionally with others.

to come back next week. Today we are makeing maps of the United States. a lots of boys and girls were out last week. Carl was the only one in his row. If you don't hurry and come to st school you will not so know very much

The next writing is that of a mature ten year old boy, this chosen for its unusual upright slant and over-developed upper zone. Here is a most imaginative child who, unless he develops some forward movement into the world could be starting a life of unproductive fantasy. The spacing between the words already shows aloofness, but the strong t-bars, clarity of form and strong middle zone are indicators that he is sociable and goal-oriented.

I hope you do to, Some news Dick S. had to stay after yesterday when I was gone. Danny hopes that you will come back some. Donald S. and Danny are going after Billy P.

This sample is that of an immature boy of ten, who is quite disorganized, undisciplined, and unable to concentrate. The downward long t-bars and pastiosity, rightward slant and disregard for the first capital letter proclaim an uncontrollable emotional intensity on the level of a temper-tantrum prone two year old. His self image is amazingly consistent for so undisciplined a hand, and all three personal pronoun I's show jealousy. The writing looks fast but the writer burnt himself out in one-third of the space taken by other members of the class. The bent strokes indicate nervous tension. Such penmanship exhibits very inconsistent upbringing and tension in the home.

are you geting any better? I hope so. I hope you will be back soon. I hope you will like these letters.

This next sample is chosen to show a lack of motor control; the functions of the eye and hand are not sufficiently co-ordinated. Like the previous child this boy has a tense and emotional nature, but the extreme cracking, bending, twisting, patching and snarling of the strokes goes beyond emotional instability and into muscle problems as well. The writing is light and thin and there are many pale sketchy strokes where the pen has grazed the paper seeking a way to control the next movement. This could be the writing of a hyper-active child.

[handwriting sample]

The final sample is a classic case of depression. The small, ragged, neglected letters move across the page without punctuation or capitals, with weak and uneven pressure and many mistakes. These problems could be aggravated by poor eyesight. The even spacing and often clear letter forms show the boy's desire to communicate and to cooperate, but emotionally he is crushed.

[handwriting sample]

The tremendous individuality of grade school children is astonishing. The child cannot separate his emotional feeling from anything he does; it takes years to develop the defenses that enable the adult to cope. Keep a collection of the writings of your children over their formative years. Objective analysis of these can give a parent many helpful insights.

THE CHILD AND AUTHORITY

The child's world starts at home with his mother and father, sisters and brothers, then broadens to school where he spends more than half of each day with the teacher. How does he view these authority figures? What are his fears, and what defenses does he develop to deal with the people and situations in his life? Ultimately, what does the child think of himself? Clues to childhood attitudes are to be seen in certain specific characteristics of his handwriting.

ATTITUDE TOWARD PARENTS.
    Personal Pronoun I . . . variations in form and slant . . .
    Size of written words, "mother" and "father" . . .
    Mistakes on those words . . . confusion . . . hostility

[handwriting sample: "Mother and father"]

LACKS RESPECT FOR AUTHORITY.

A dont like tRicks

Overinflated K's . . . capitals out of place . . . rebellious nature . . . discipline problem.

TEMPER TANTRUMS.

dont kill it dead

Ticklike strokes . . . heavy slashed i-dots . . . blobs and pastiosity . . . downward t-bars to right of stem . . . maniac d . . . temper often a protective device. A domineering attitude often covers for child's feelings of inadequacy.

SPIRITUAL DEVELOPMENT . . . NO SENSE OF GUILT.

Breakfast tastes bad today

Upper loops that are consistently made the same height as lower-case letters . . . wobbly base line . . . upbringing at fault. A combination of high and stunted upper loops shows lack of spiritual development.

WARPED OR TWISTED THINKING.

Upper loops appear dented.

DECEIT.

war kills many

A's and O's have double loops. Fear of punishment causes child to lie; he will mislead others when it suits his purpose. With acquisitiveness (initial hooks) could become a thief.

JEALOUSY.

mice like cheeses

Pinched loops in child's writing or s-stroke that returns leftward.

RESTLESSNESS.

sunny days are for play

Lower loops appear extremely long; confusion results when there is tangling. Athletic p = loop on bottom.

TENSION.

our house has three bedrooms and a big porch

Concentration is found in small writing. This intensifies every other trait in personality. Very small writing suggests unnatural tension. Child is being overpowered with guilt . . . must relax.

INDEPENDENCE.

our daily bread

Short d and t stems . . . pride is long retraced d stem.

DETECTING CHILDHOOD FEARS AND UNDERLYING INSECURITIES

FEAR OF FAILURE/GUILTY COVER-UP.

Thank you for

give me one

Slow, careful, retouched . . . rigid writing with conservatism and restraint.

FEAR OF BEING ALONE.

My favorite toy is the cannon I got for my birthday

Crowding . . . touching zones . . . writing confined to limited space on the paper.

FEAR OF THE FUTURE/LIVING IN THE PAST.

Gloria is my friend

Back to self strokes . . . cover strokes . . . left tending lead-ins (dependency).

THE DEPENDENT CHILD.

many dogs go away

Immature lead-in strokes . . . lower loops drawn to left.

AFRAID TO START.

lets not fight

Small i's are dotted and t's are crossed to the left of the stem.

UNCOMFORTABLE AROUND OTHERS/
SELF-CONSCIOUS.

plants and animals

Last hump of m and n rises and/or is crushed to left. Child is insecure and cannot relax and accept himself . . . inferiority complex . . . aloof.

SHY.

I'd rather not if thats o.k.

Small and left-slanting.

DISTRUST OF OTHERS.

safty first is always good

Small pinched loops on the end of a down stroke on g and y show clannishness. Child selects only few friends.

Inflexible initial strokes indicate resentment toward real or imagined imposition. Child has learned to suspect others' motives.

dont try to walk home with me

Stubbornness can be seen in brace-like tee-pees. Child resists domination by others.

DEPRESSION/GLOOM/PESSIMISM.

then and my bike dad said broke we

Downhill and/or disintegrated forms are evidence of many inner fears and discouragement.

FEAR OF DISAPPROVAL.

tall soldiers would be dead

Fat loops in d's and t's. Child fears criticism which he interprets as rejection . . . hypersensitive.

FEELS UNWORTHY/LOW GOALS.

I think that auntie went

Low-crossed t's in which the bar runs into the lower-case letters. Rejection and disapproval of parents causes this in child.

HIDES FEELINGS/REPRESSION.

looking for my kitty

Retracing. Child afraid to show true feelings . . . suffers inwardly . . . due to early trauma like loss of love.

I want to go too

Looped finals on ovals. The insecure child resorts to secrecy to hide his feelings . . . feelings often buried.

CHILDHOOD DEFENSES AND PROTECTIVE MEASURES AND THE CHILD'S SELF-IMAGE

DEFENSIVE GUILT FEELINGS.

our car broke down

Drawing strokes into ovals of o's, a's, d's and g's reveals guilty feelings, a defense against inadequacy child feels.

AVOIDS FACING REALITY.

someone made me do it

Bloated upper zone or initial loops on ovals. Disturbed child escapes through self-deceit . . . rationalizes . . . evasive . . . ready excuses.

FANTASY WORLD.

The cat wont eat

T bars float above stem . . . tall letters emphasized. Child escapes into daydreams to avoid harsh realities.

CLINGING FOR SECURITY.

our car trips took much too long

Final hooks on words. Child fears changes and clings to secure past; also note leftward slant and excessive lead-ins.

ALWAYS TRIES TO PLEASE.

pretty fish swim slow in our pond

Lower case p's and s's appear to sprawl weakly in script. Child always gives in in effort to gain approval and love.

THE NATURAL DIPLOMAT.

naturally became of raining weather

Handwriting progressively tapers off. Child avoids controversy; can hide true feelings if necessary to gain ends.

THE SHOW-OFF.

Danny police help us

Finals tend to rise above lower-case letters. Excessive ornamentation and flourishes which compensate often for feelings of inadequacy.

ATTITUDE TOWARD SELF.

I know what you are doing you are reading your letter from me.

A combination of personal pronoun I and clear consistent form level, slant and good rhythm. At left is a mature sixth grader.

sandbanks best I think en winter

Fluctuations in writing slant. Child's self-confidence easily lost and regained.

I hope I will get first

Reliable consistent confidence.

I like my bike. I ride it.

Feels superior. I and UZ letters reach high; also can mean small attention to everyday affairs. fairs.

CHILDHOOD HANDWRITING PROFILE I

Here are three samples of a boy's handwriting spanning ages 11 to 20 which show how a constrained and outwardly dutiful youngster becomes a most individual adult. The discipline of school and everyday duties was not comfortable or natural to this personality and it quite literally exploded.

The 11 year old reproduces the sixth grade penmanship model below with great slowness and pressure and excessive care. He is rigorously constricting himself out of desire to please and to fit into formal expectations.

I realize how important it is to improve the quality of my writing and develop an easy flowing style in joining the letters! I know that the exercises in this book will

Four years later, a sophomore in high school, he has rebelled against the strictures of the model and employs large, bouncy, disconnected print-writing with many rebellious capital letters jumping up.

I WON'T HAVE ANY "B" AVERAGE '; AS A MATTER OF FACT I FIGURE I'LL BE STUCK IN STUDY HALL ALL

Again four years later, at the age of 20, the writer has settled down considerably in size, showing a willingness to concentrate, but the letter forms are even more fragmented and original. The even baselines and spacing are evidence of his moral and social sense, but the form quality marks him as highly independent and impatient of authority, the mundane, and details.

I wouldt wamther I smam join the
navy. Being a soldier or sailer
zoom is nothing like playing
classion war-games or being a
classion soldier-sailer. chances me,

CHILDHOOD HANDWRITING PROFILE II

This group of seven samples in close sequence profiles a girl from the age of 12 to 20. The first three samples at twelve years were written the same summer and demonstrate the changeability of adolescent slant and size, and the uneven baseline, a variety that almost obscures the basically consistent rhythm and letter forms.

but its not only that I really like camp o if I left now I couldn't have learned and had half as much Riding/hr. Art/hr Rec Swim, ±hr. Mommie & think that & might want the extra riding cause & really like it, there haven't been there since the family excursion when I was real little + got that Kimono. After this I'm heading towards Bakersfield to see all. If I see any of your old buddies I'll tell them you said hi (even if you didn't)!

At the age of 15 the self-image letter I is written two different ways, the independent pedestal form and a self-enclosed and protective circle. The slant draws to the left; the baseline is settling down.

infirmary with it. I'll probably be put In it later but & had alot of work to do today so I'm in

A year later at sixteen the personal pronoun is consistently self-absorbed and circular, slant has moved to the vertical, and there are more connections, more unusual letter forms and more attention to appearance on the page.

The phone call I don't remember having called San Francisco at all... except when we were in Palto alto I might have but

At the age of 17 the hand begins its rightward movement. The personal pronoun has emerged from a circle into a rebellious and self-conscious small letter i. Loops, flourishes, and felon's claws are disappearing, giving way to underlying maturity and efficiency of form.

one made a bet up someone else that i wouldn't make it thru the semister. i laughed when i heard but in reality

Three years later at the age of 20 the writing has taken on its mature characteristics with the exception of a still unsettled lower zone, the area most prone to change form throughout life. The script now covers the paper, the baseline rises, slant is rightward, manifesting energy, enthusiasm, and the intent to make an impression on life.

I am doing a damn good job of funds together. just because I ran into this month doesn't mean I didn't scrimp.

THE HANDWRITING OF ADOLESCENTS

Up to the time of puberty, that is, the period at which sexual maturity is reached, most children's handwriting strives to emulate school-imposed forms. Starting, however, about the 12th to 14th year, as physical maturity begins to accelerate, the child's writing form breaks into confusion. Loose loops, blotches, uneven baselines, varied slant, stabs of pressure, extravagant formations reflect both inward tension and impulsive, exuberant acting-out. Often signs of guilt, emotional tension, or overcontrol appear as the adolescent copes with developing sexual drives and characteristics, trying to fit into the restraints of authority and still be himself. For a demonstration of this energy and individuality, pass a junior high as classes let out. Most adults feel engulfed and overwhelmed.

Just as girls were about two years ahead of the boys in motor development in grade school, so their sexual maturation occurs sooner, close to 12 years of age. The average boy matures around 14. As the adolescent years (12 to 15 or so) proceed, the rate of sexual maturation difference diminishes. Normally, there are no significant differences remaining by the age of 18. Emotional maturity is, of course, a longer and harder-won process. But by 18 the handwriting can be expected to have settled down and taken on most of its life-long qualities.

Writing pressure tends to decline progressively as children advance through elementary school and levels off around 12 years. A brief pressure break occurs about the 17th year when pressure drops to an unprecedented low, reflecting the sudden release of tension after puberty. Within less than a year, however, pressure returns to the writer's natural level. (These pressure changes have been recorded in psychological studies using special pressure-sensitive writing tools.)

All this is to say that parent and teacher should expect rhythmic disturbance in adolescent writing; only when the imbalance or its opposite, unnatural rigidity, persist into maturity is there cause for alarm. Also, adolescents often imitate the writing characteristics of someone whom they admire, and they like to experiment with writing fads and embellishments like the circle i dot and special signatures. Quite usually there is a period of trying out different slants, the reclined writing being a favorite, before the personality finds its own individual expression.

Once allowance is made for adolescent emotionalism and exaggeration, analyzing writing of this age group is like analyzing adult writing in terms of strokes, shapes, zones and rhythm. The sample below is that of an energetic and extroverted girl of 15 who still lacks control over her feelings and needs a lot of emotional room. The puffed-up capitals, pastiosity, uneven pressure, slant and letter size will settle down. This satisfactory adjustment is predicted by the presence of good t-bars, smooth contracting strokes, fairly disciplined baselines with little tangling for so much crowding, also legibility, and few lead-ins.

Note the felon's claw which shows the presence of guilt. Such a writer will provoke others, consciously or unconsciously depending upon the zone in which it is found, in order to be punished by another's anger. In adolescent writings it is also the sign of a desire to form cliques, clubs, close and secure groups of special friends, what graphologists call "clannishness."

The following writing is that of a hard-working, responsible 15 year old boy, who is making a cautious and controlled transition to adulthood. He is trying very hard to govern his moods and to meet all expectations; notice how the baseline moves up or down as he stops to consider what he will write next. No impulsiveness or exuberance here, he is rather too close to the model to be lively company, but with the garlands and loops it is a friendly and feeling script.

P. S. I hope that this isn't to much of a personal nature but could you tell me how I stand with you?

DISTURBED ADOLESCENTS

Not all young people make a smooth transition to maturity. The 16 year old girl writing below is the classic follower for better or for worse, lacking any standards or determination of her own. The dished t-bars, drooping garlands and pale pressure illustrate the victim. Note also the vacillating baseline, uneven spacing, and slow awkward letter forms. Although a friendly and kind garlanded script, she will seek approval of any kind and cannot say no.

going up there early tomorrow morning. I will get smashed with Kathy and some friends at which point we will stumble over to Campus

The 16 year old boy in the next sample has already served time in prison for a violent crime. The handwriting pressure is uneven and heavy, the forms muddy and clubbed, with slashing angry strokes and an unstable slant and baseline.

The silly bucket stood there That had so long been busted I dreamt that they took it And when I awoke I laughed

Tips and Guidelines for Doing Your Own Analysis

When you meet someone new and are curious about him or her, don't be shy—ask for a sample. Most people feel pleased that you are interested in them and are eager to hear what you have to say.

When you have this opportunity of getting the sample yourself, get it on unlined paper so the writer can choose the spacing. We recommend you use a consistent size and weight of paper; this will enable you to get an accurate size, spacing and pressure comparison between samples.

To ensure yourself the most accurate analysis possible, have the writer use a ballpoint pen. These pens or very sharp pencils show many aspects of writing that a felt tip pen or dull pencil will blur. Some individuals have a favorite pen they always use. If so, let them use it, because such a preference will give you additional information. The best colors of ink for future reproduction purposes are black and red, while blue doesn't photocopy well at all. Keep this in mind, for one day you may want to make copies of some of your samples.

Ask your writers to pen at least two paragraphs, sign and date the sample. Some people find it easy to think of something to say, while others don't know what to write and get nervous. (Already this tells you something.) To help, you can suggest they write a letter to themselves relating something they've seen or done recently, or describe what they see around them at the moment, or you can dictate something. Tell them that it really doesn't matter what they say—which it doesn't—and that you will be analyzing *how* they write, not the content itself.

In fact, when you observe a writing, it is a good idea not to read it until you have received your graphological impressions based on the look of the writing. Often the verbal content is distracting or even false (people will sometimes try to fool you), and to read the sample too soon may reduce the accuracy of your interpretation.

Somewhere on the sample make a note of the date on which it was written and the age, sex and handedness of the writer. This is pertinent information that can't usually be determined from the writing, and you'll find it valuable to your analysis and in building your collection of samples.

When the writer or someone who knows him well is present for the analysis, be sure to jot down whatever personal information you receive as you progress. The graphological facts will always be there to see, but the personal history of the writer can only be told by him or by those who are acquainted with him. Staple this information to the sample.

You'll be tempted to mark on your samples as you make observations. Don't do it. It alters the original clarity. Instead, we suggest the tracing paper method. Place a sheet about the same size over the sample and affix it with staples or tape. Then on that surface you can circle any traits that seem unusual, draw lines to determine slant, underline words or phrases that stand out—all without changing your sample from its original condition.

Establish a good filing system right from the start. Some people prefer to file alphabetically by name, others do so by personal association such as family. Another good system is to file by outstanding traits revealed by the writing, such as violence, instability, conventionality, illness, dishonesty, or by rhythmic disturbance, inflated loops or zonal extremes. It doesn't matter what system you use, as long as it provides you access to that certain sample when you want to see it.

When you are doing someone's analysis and other people are present, respect the privacy and feelings of the writer. If you are alone with the person, you have the opportunity to be more specific. Most people will ask to hear the bad things about themselves as well as the good things, but may not wish to hear them in front of others.

Most of the time, it will be the writing itself which will tell you what tone to take as you deliver your analysis. A very rightward slant with a tall, loopy d and a vulnerable personal pronoun I warns you of an extremely sensitive nature. Be aware of this. Use tact in your delivery. On the other hand, a vertical slant with many stick figures and strong pressure shows you a writer who can roll with the punches.

Practice analyzing your own writing. Whenever something new appears, think about how you are feeling as you write. You'll learn a lot this way.

Always be honest. If you see characteristics you don't wish to discuss, avoid doing so, but don't be tempted to flatter the writer at the expense of graphological truth.

PROCEDURE FOR ANALYSIS

The observation chart on the following pages is meant for your use as an aid in doing analysis. We suggest you make copies of these pages before using them so you will always have blanks to work with.

First, scan the sample for a few minutes without writing anything down. Keep yourself open and try not to focus on any particular formation. How do you react to the writing? Once you have received an overall impact of impressions, begin to notice what it is about the writing that makes it different—uniquely its own. Look for extremes, such as very small or very large writing, bizarre spacing, unusual formations, odd proportions, erratic pressure or slant. Make a note of these. The importance of your first impressions can't be overemphasized. Often they are amazingly accurate.

Now you are ready to use your checklist of characteristics. As you examine your sample, place a check next to each characteristic that fits. You should contemplate the checklist before trying to come to any conclusion about what each trait means. When you have finished, go back to the beginning of the list and jot down the personal meaning associated with the graphological traits you've found. You should always be aware that one trait can modify or shade the meaning of another. The writing as a whole picture is more important than any tiny detail.

HANDWRITING ANALYSIS OBSERVATION CHART

Name: _____ Age: _____ Sex: _____ Date of Sample: _____

First Impressions, overall look, personal reactions, graphological extremes:

_____

Systematic Checklist: Check all the characteristics you can observe in each area.

ZONES - Indicators of inner balance and character.
_____ balanced
_____ dominating UZ
_____ dominating MZ
_____ dominating LZ
_____ dominating UZ and LZ
_____ erratic proportion
      additional zonal observations:

BASELINE - Measure of temperament, mood level and quality of social control.
_____ straight
_____ rigid
_____ sinuous
_____ rising
_____ falling
      other observations:

SLANT - Social orientation and degree of emotional expression.
_____ vertical
_____ inclined
_____ very·inclined
_____ extremely inclined
_____ reclined
_____ very reclined
_____ extremely reclined
_____ unstable
      additional slant observations:

PRESSURE - Intensity of energy, how displayed, sensuality of the writer.

_____ heavy

_____ medium

_____ light

_____ average width

_____ thick

_____ thin

_____ shaded

_____ pastiose

_____ very pastiose

_____ sharp

additional pressure observations:

SIZE - Emphasis placed by the writer on his own importance.

_____ average

_____ large

_____ small

_____ variable

_____ other size observations

SPACING - Relationship between the writer and other people or situations.

_____ narrow letters

_____ wide letters

_____ letters close together

_____ letters wide apart

_____ words close together

_____ words wide apart

_____ lines close together

_____ lines far apart

_____ tangling between lines

_____ rigid spacing

_____ irregular spacing

_____ wide margins

_____ narrow margins

other margin observations:

other spatial observations:

SPEED - Mental and physical agility.

_____ fast

_____ slow

RHYTHM and FORM QUALITY - Balance and harmony within the self and between the self and the world at large; personal style of expression.

_____ good rhythm
_____ bad rhythm
_____ embellished
_____ simplified
_____ neglected
  other rhythmic observations:

  other form level observations:

STROKES and SHAPES - Qualities of activity, thought, expression and communication.
Overall look:
_____ round
_____ angular
_____ threaded
_____ mixed

_____ loops - what kind?
_____ stick-figure strokes
Ovals:
_____ open
_____ closed
_____ knotted
_____ lead-ins - what kind?
_____ endings - what kind?
Connecting Strokes:
_____ garland
_____ arcaded
_____ angular
_____ threaded
_____ mixed
_____ very connected writing
_____ mostly connected writing
_____ disconnected writing
_____ totally disconnected writing
_____ printing
  other observations:

What do you observe about the following:
      personal pronoun "I":

      small letter "d":

      t-bars:

      i-dots:

      the signature:

      capital letter formations:

      small letter formations:

      the "y" and the "g":

Are there signs of emotional distress?

Are there signs of dishonesty?

Any other special considerations?

SUMMATION:

Bibliography

GENERAL REFERENCE

Bunker, M. N. *Handwriting Analysis - The Science of Determining Personality by Graphoanalysis.* Nelson-Hall Co., Publishers, 1974. Founder, International Graphoanalysis Society. Uneven and chatty.

Falcon, Hal, Ph.D. *How to Analyze Handwriting.* Trident Press. 1964. General anecdotal discussion with chapters on determining whether one is eye, ear, or action-minded.

French, William Leslie. *Graphoanalysis - Your Handwriting and What It Means.* Newcastle Publishing Co., 1974. Vague and chatty with samples of famous people.

Hartford, Huntington. *You Are What You Write.* Macmillan Publishing Co. Inc., 1973. Mr. Hartford is the founder of The Handwriting Institute in New York City. Summarizes leading graphologists through history. Recommended.

Jacoby, H. J. *Analysis of Handwriting - An Introduction to Scientific Graphology.* George Allen & Unwin Ltd., 1968. Chapters on children, criminology, vocational guidance. Not enough samples for illustration.

Le Guen, Monique. *Graphology.* Media Books S.A. Nyon, 1976. Visually elegant book with unusual chapter on international handwriting styles.

Marcuse, Irene, Ph.D. *Guide to Personality Through Your Handwriting.* Arco Publishing Company, Inc. 1974. Children and adolescents, mental disorders, criminal tendencies. Special section on famous composers through history.

Olyanova, Nadya. *Handwriting Tells.* Wilshire Book Company, 1973. Intuitive and experienced woman. Recommended.

Olyanova, Nadya. *The Psychology of Handwriting - Secrets of Handwriting Analysis.* Wilshire Book Company, 1973. Many examples by famous personalities. Chapters on emotional and physical illness. Recommended.

Rosen, Billie Pesin. *The Science of Handwriting Analysis - A Guide to Character and Personality.* Paperback Library, Inc., 1968. Chapters on Criminology. Recommended.

Smith, Albert J. *Applied Graphology - A Textbook on Character Analysis From Handwriting.* The Gregg Publishing Company, 1920. Appendix gives personality traits alphabetically with corresponding writing traits.

Solomon, Shirl. *How to Really Know Yourself Through Your Handwriting.* Taplinger Publishing Company, 1973. An individual approach to letter formation through geometric symbols - circle, triangle, square and squiggle.

Teltscher, Dr. Herry O. *Handwriting, Revelation of Self - A Source Book of Psychographology.* Hawthorn Books, 1971. Touches on children's writings, personnel selection, criminology, growth and decline of personality.

INTRODUCTORY

Holder, Robert. *You Can Analyze Handwriting - A Practical Tool for Self-knowledge and Personal Power.* Wilshire Book Company, 1974. Lists general personality types with corresponding writing traits.

Hughes, Albert E. *Self-analysis From Your Handwriting.* Grosset & Dunlap, 1966. Chapters on intelligence, unreliability and dishonesty.

Marley, John. *Handwriting Analysis Made Easy.* Wilshire Book Co., 1976. Very basic with lists of positive and negative personality traits.

Martin, Renee. *Your Script is Showing.* Western Publishing Co., Inc., 1969.

Meyer, Jerome S. *The Handwriting Analyzer.* Simon & Schuster, 1974. Workbook format with tables and charts - especially good one on letter specifics.

Paterson, Jane. *Interpreting Handwriting.* David McKay Company Inc., 1976. Precisely presented basic format.

Sara, Dorothy. *Personality and Penmanship - A Guide to Handwriting Analysis.* H.C. Publishers, Inc., 1969. Very simplistic. A chapter on doodles.

TECHNICAL

Allport, Gordon. *Studies in Expressive Movement.* The Macmillan Company, 1933.

Mendel, A. O. *Personality in Handwriting - A Handbook of American Graphology.* Stephen Daye Press, New York, 1947. Chapters on psychopathology plus a section by Alfred Kanfer on physiology and pathology. Recommended.

Pulver, Max. *Symbolism of Handwriting.* Orell Fussli Verlag, 1931. Gives a symbolic meaning to the writing space.

Roman, Klara. *The Encyclopedia of the Written Word - A Lexicon for Graphology and Other Aspects of Writing.* Frederick Ungar Publishing Co., 1968. Dictionary format combines definition with discussion.

Roman, Klara. *Handwriting, A Key to Personality.* Noonday Press, 1952. Chapters on children and adolescents. Mrs. Roman is a Ph.D. in psychology and has taught graphology at the New School for Social Research, New York. Highly recommended.

Saudek, Robert. *The Psychology of Handwriting.* George Allen and Unwin Ltd., 1925.

Sonnemann, Ulrich, Ph.D. *Handwriting Analysis as a Psychodiagnostic Tool.* Grune and Stratton, Inc. 1950. Professor at The New School for Social Research, New York. Complex and rewarding. Highly recommended.

Wolff, Werner, Ph.D. *Diagrams of the Unconscious - Handwriting and Personality in Measurement, Experiment and Analysis.* Grune & Stratton, 1948. Pioneer work with signatures. Professor of Psychology, Bard College, Annandale-on-Hudson. Technical but excellent.

SPECIAL INTEREST

Currer-Briggs, Noel, Kennett, Brian, and Patterson, Jane. *Handwriting Analysis in Business - The Use of Graphology in Personnel Selection.* Associated Business Programmes, 1971. Excellent samples and analysis.

De Sainte Colombe, Paul. *Grapho-Therapeutics: The Pen and Pencil Therapy.* Popular Library 1972. How to change your personality through handwriting.

Friedenhain, Paula. *Write and Reveal - Interpretation of Handwriting.* Peter Owen Ltd. Saudek's technique of analysis with chapters on the writing and drawing of deaf and normal children.

Green, Jane Nugent. *You and Your Private I - Graphological Analysis focused on the Personal Pronoun I.* Llewellyn Publications, 1975.

Holder, Robert. *Sex, Health and Your Handwriting.* Award Books, New York, 1971. A very generalized text with good samples.

Kaminsky, A. R. *Behold: the Inner Universe of Handwriting.* O'Sullivan Woodside and Company, 1974. Personal anecdotes by a man who can construct physical appearance from handwriting.

Marcuse, Irene. *Guide to the Disturbed Personality Through Handwriting.* Arco Publishing Co., 1969.

Moretti, Girolamo. *The Saints Through Their Handwriting.* The Macmillan Company, 1964. Catholic bias.

Pelton, Robert W. *Handwriting and Drawings Reveal Your Child's Personality.* Hawthorn Books, Inc. 1973.

Solomon, Shirl. *Knowing Your Child Through His Handwriting and Drawings.* Crown Publishers. Inc. New York. 1978.

Index

Page numbers for the handwriting
examples are printed in italics.